PROTECTING YOUR INNER PEACE

Staying Peaceful in Challenging Situations

J. MICHAEL GOULDING
MSW, LCSW

outskirtspress
DENVER, COLORADO

The opinions expressed in this manuscript are solely the opinions of the author and do not represent the opinions or thoughts of the publisher. The author has represented and warranted full ownership and/or legal right to publish all the materials in this book.

Protecting Your Inner Peace
Staying Peaceful in Challenging Situations
All Rights Reserved.
Copyright © 2013 J. Michael Goulding MSW, LCSW
v4.0

Cover Photo © 2013 Dave Goulding Portrait. All rights reserved- use with permission. Illustrations © 2013 Julie Macie. All rights reserved - use with permission. Aikido Illustrations © 2013 Deborah McDuffie. All rights reserved - use with permission.

This book may not be reproduced, transmitted, or stored in whole or in part by any means, including graphic, electronic, or mechanical without the express written consent of the publisher except in the case of brief quotations embodied in critical articles and reviews.

Outskirts Press, Inc.
http://www.outskirtspress.com

ISBN: 978-1-4787-1861-1

Outskirts Press and the "OP" logo are trademarks belonging to Outskirts Press, Inc.

PRINTED IN THE UNITED STATES OF AMERICA

The Art of Peace begins with you. Work on yourself and your appointed task in the Art of Peace. Everyone has a spirit that can be refined, a body that can be trained in some manner, a suitable path to follow. You are here for no other purpose than to realize your inner divinity and manifest your innate enlightenment. Foster peace in your own life and then apply the Art to all that you encounter.

– Oh Sensei, Founder of Aikido

For all people committed to peace ~

Table of Contents

Introduction i
Part 1: Sorting It All Out 1
   Why Inner Peace? 2
   What is Your Peaceful State? 4
   Barriers to Your Inner Peace 6
   Making Peace with Warriors 12
   The "Warriors" or Martial Artists I Know 13
   Historical Warriors Show Compassion 14
   Peace is Even Effective in War 15
   World War I Assessments, Examples of
   Compassion by the Military, 1917 16
   Nation Building Effort 17
   Coming Full Circle 18
   A Martial Arts Metaphor for Peace 18
   5 Strategies for Protecting Your Inner Peace 19
      1. Sorting it all out 19
      2. Protecting yourself 19
      3. Making sure you are heard 19
      4. Forming alliances 19
      5. Seeing things as they are 19
   Sorting it All Out 19

My First Master Teacher - Liu Siong - Willem Reeders 25
Morihei Ueshiba-O'Sensei 26
What is Aikido? 26
What is the Space Inside Our Personal
Circle and How does this Tie into Aikido? 27
Addictions 34
Benefits of the Peaceful Life 36

Part 2: Protecting Yourself From Others 40
Blocks & Evading 40
Evade, Align, Enter 41
Personal Policy 44
Monkey in the Middle 47
Get Out of the Crossfire! 50
Strikes 54
Snake Past the Head Games (Tenshinage Irimi) 56
Wait Them Out (Karate Kid) 59
Expose the Inconsistency (Ryotedori Irimi) 61
Pre-Emptive Strike on Repeated Attacks.
(Morning Phone Calls) 64
If I was Your Favorite Brother, Uncle, Sister…
(Cradle Irimi) 67
Go Straight for the Emotions 70
Yield and Overcome (Picking Up the Penny) 72
Natural Consequences 75

Part 3: Alliances 78
Relationships – Forming Alliances 79
What is Validation? 82
Alliance Exercise 85
When is it Safe to Let Others In?' 89
Entering Other People's Circles 93
Being a Good Friend 93

Tips for Being a Good Friend 94
Take Responsibility for Your Part 94
Use "I" Statements 96
Empathize with the Other Person's Circle 98
Conflict Resolution: When Circles Collide *99*
Seven Steps to Successfully Manage A Conflict: 100
Children and Your Circle 105

Part 4: The Mirror – Seeing Things As They Are 108
Adding Meaning to Neutral Words 108
Reflection 112
The Emerald Tablet: As Below, So Above 112
Ways the Mirror Impacts Our World 113
How Do You Create a Mirror within Yourself? 116
Goals 116
Seeking a Feeling of Spiritual Cleansing 118
Meditation/Prayer 119
Art 120
Moving Meditation 120
Purging Your Physical Possessions 120
Get Right with Yourself 121
Explore Your Snap Judgments 121
Forgiveness 122
Dignity 123
Strategies to Use Physically to be More at Peace 124
Guard the Senses 125
Organize 125
Cognitive Strategies for Protecting Your Inner Peace 127
Strategies to be Emotionally More at Peace 128
Emotional Bathroom 130
Predictable Emotions 131

Emotional Storms 131
Managing the Storms 131
Oxygen Mask Rule 133
Transforming Anger into Peace 135
Shielding Yourself from Your Thoughts 140
Confronting Temptation 142
The Enemy Within 143
The Generous Benefactor Question Part I & Part II 144
Strengthen Your Position 147
Living Life with Integrity 149
Take Charge of Your Life so Others Won't! 152
The Wheel of Good Fortune 154
Balance 157
Turn on Your Radar 159
Play 159
Stopping Guilt 160
Does It Really Matter? 162
Become the Observer 162
Abandon Expectations 165
Be More Open 165
State Change 166
Create Something 167
Three Questions 167
Talk to Someone 168
The Mirror is Your Best Friend 170
The Ultimate Goal 172
Resources/References 175

Introduction

Thank you for taking the time to read this book. What that tells me is you have some interest in improving your life and you are interested in improving the lives of others. Reading a book such as this one means that you are open to the idea that there is a better way to live your life and you are willing to listen to the ideas of others. With all of these qualities present, you are ultimately contributing to a better world for all of us. This is the biggest reason for my gratitude.

My objectives for you are to save yourself time by synthesizing my 20-plus years of experience and hundreds of credit hours of scholarship into an easy to read medium designed to help you reach your true goals so you may live freely and peacefully within yourself. If you find a way to your heart's desire, you will save even more time. You will be able to reach your goals faster and find peace of mind with more fulfillment and with greater ease. By learning the techniques in this book you will discover many benefits along the way.

Don't Believe a Word That is Said

The best way for you to get the most out of this reading is for you to question what you read. What that means is I want you to challenge what is being said. Ultimately all learning is self-learning. When you challenge something does not appear to be working for you it may be that the information you are receiving is wrong OR it may mean you end up with a deeper understanding because you took the time to question. Question what is said and read on. You will likely find there is truth in this message that is answered or detailed in later chapters.

Stay Away From "I Know That"

Many times as people are reading materials they find the material is similar to something they have read in the past. This often causes many people to flip the "off" switch in their brains and they end up reading some meaning that is different than the truths actually attempting to be expressed in this writing. Being mindful of this can help you to explore a refreshing new look at some very old issues.

Walk Away with Skills You Can Use to Enhance Your Life Today!

Your time is important and many times we read books that are interesting with an entertaining twist. We may talk about them with a few friends, scratch our heads and put the books up on the shelf. There they sit, with all of the ideas that came with them. The goal of this book is to give you the tools that will actually help you move through the obstacles in your life. I have taken many of the interventions that have demonstrated success in my practice and put them here for you. I have been repeating similar messages to my clients and discovered that a little bit of information can cause great fulfillment in a person's life. Completing this book will give you coping skills to help you protect your inner peace and discover your heart's desire.

The activities in this book are present to assist you in internalizing the concepts it presents. If you feel that you get the concepts, and the activities will only slow you down, then do what brings you the most emotional fulfillment without feeling a sense of obligation. I do feel that in order to fully understand the concepts of the book it would be beneficial for you to do the circle exercise. My goal is that you actually walk away with a new perspective and the skills to make your life a more fulfilling one. May you find your inner peace so we all can enjoy a more peaceful planet!

PART 1
SORTING IT ALL OUT

How I Came Up with The Idea of this Book

People talk about ideas hitting them as some metaphor, but the idea for this book hit me. When I say it hit me, I mean I actually got the idea for this book after someone hit me in the head.

During my teenage years I was in a martial arts class working on a technique where someone was supposed to throw a punch close enough to perform a blocking move and counter attack. During the exercise my partner threw a punch that glanced off the side of my head. Like a blip on a radar screen, my kung-fu teacher appeared at my side to ask me the question, "Whose fault was it?"

I was smart enough to realize that whenever someone asks whose fault something is, it usually means it is my fault. I confessed it was my fault and my teacher explained how I could not control what other people do. He went on to explain how

I was responsible for protecting the space around my body. This concept always stuck with me and made a lot of sense to me. It became even more apparent as became a therapist. Instead of warding off kicks and strikes, I learned to defend myself from people trying to place their responsibilities on me. As I got older I realized people have been reporting about this mysterious space that we all intuitively grasp. I learned the importance of focusing on taking care of my personal space.

Little did I know in that moment dwelled the secret of inner peace. That secret is shifting my efforts from trying to change the circumstances of the outside world to learning how to keep myself at peace, regardless of world circumstances. I learned that first lesson of keeping my physical self safe through martial arts and then I was able to apply the same idea to my verbal interactions with people as I grew in my skills as a licensed mental health therapist. I learned that it was important to change my verbal interactions with others so I could protect myself and, at the same time, keep my peace with others.

Why Inner Peace?

After listening to people's stories for over 20 years I have determined that the universal goal people are seeking is peace. People may use other words to describe peace, but ultimately it is peace that they are seeking. Some of the ways that people articulate the peace that they want is by describing such things as wanting more money, a loving relationship, better job or better health. Whatever the goal is, it relates to peace.

As John F. Kennedy so eloquently put it in his speech on peace given at the American University:

"What kind of peace do we seek? Not a Pax Americana enforced on the world by American weapons of war. Not the peace of the grave or the security of the slave. I am talking about genuine peace, the kind of peace that makes life on earth worth living, the kind that enables men and nations to grow and to hope and to build a better life for their children—not merely peace for Americans but peace for all men and women—not merely peace in our time but peace for all time."

Kennedy does not directly say what peace is in his speech, but one can get a sense that peace is an ultimate goal that creates a good life. Kennedy mentions the positive effects of peace and what it can do for our lives and our world. Kennedy also talks about what peace is not. Peace reveals itself to be an important byproduct of what you get when you remove what is not peaceful. Take away pain, suffering, hunger, resistance, poverty and loneliness. What is left after that all of this is taken away from you is peace.

Whether your goal is prosperity, freedom, good health or love, you can trace each of these endeavors back to peace. Prosperity is peace from lack, freedom is peace from slavery to anything, good health is peace from pain and love is peace from loneliness.

Peace is not easy to define, but we all have a sense of what it is. I define peace as having a direct connection to your highest self regardless of outside circumstances. Everyone has a different definition of a highest self. It could be however you perceive your God or being all that you can be, if you do not believe in a higher power. Peace also includes an element of acceptance of the circumstances life gives you, If there is an unpleasant circumstance in your life, then you do not pretend it to be different or better than it is. By seeing the situation as it is you are able to make the changes to maintain peace in your life.

What is Your Peaceful State?

Remember a time when you were in a blissful state as a child. Maybe it was some place in nature or playing hide and go seek at someone's house. Maybe it was just hanging out in the corner of a courtyard. There was not a care in the world except for building the sandcastle, drawing a picture in chalk or seeing how many blocks you could stack up. There were endless experiences jumping into a pile of leaves, watching a stream or lying on the grass looking up at the clouds. There were no agendas, multitasking or assignments ahead of you. Every experience was rich with life. The skies were bluer, the sunsets were more golden and the blades of grass were greener.

Now imagine an adult version of this. You are on the beach or in the mountains enjoying your favorite secluded area with the person/people of your choice, even if that person is just you. There is not a care in the world. Your bills are paid. You have plenty of money in savings. There is only a healthy body. Your kids are with their favorite person, someone who takes the best care of them, or they are with you having the time of their lives. Everything at work was taken care of before you left on your trip, with plenty of good signs ahead for when you get back, yet no projects to start. In other words, you have nothing to worry about. Nothing has to be done and you can focus all of your attention on the present moment in your favorite place. This is the state of inner peace that is our natural state. We function best physically, emotionally and spiritually when we are in this state of peace. This is the closest state to being what we truly are inside. There are different ideas as to what that is, but for now I will call it true spirit.

Realistically many of us do not have the luxury of having that level of peace all of the time. We have people who are demanding time from us, as well as physical ailments and obligations that weigh on our minds. We have people who sit near us who talk too loud about negative issues without respecting our space. The weather can be too hot or too cold, with unexpected gusts of wind. The external world, though, is not nearly as bad as our internal world, what we do to ourselves. We obsess over all of the other things we could be doing to fulfill our obligations to others. Maybe there was a birthday or wedding to attend during that same week. We sit there and beat ourselves up about taking time off when we should be doing something to contribute to our financial situation instead adding to our debt. These are the things that block our spirit. If you do not believe in spirit then think of it as conflicting with your true emotions.

When counseling others, I have come to the conclusion that it all comes down to feelings. It is emotions that are the driving force behind anything. To demonstrate this point I will use the common example of people having the desire to have more money. On the surface, it looks as if material gain is the motivating force behind this desire. The reality, in most cases, is that people are seeking freedom, security, popularity and power. These can be the benefits of having more money, but they are emotionally based. Feeling free can be joyful. Security can give you a sense of emotional peace. You can achieve these emotions without having a lot of money. Conversely, you can have a lot of money by being married to someone rich, abusive and controlling. The end result would likely be the opposite of feeling freedom, security, popularity and power, despite having a lot of money.

Exercise
1. Write down what emotions you want to have more of in your life. Likely examples of these emotions would be joy, happiness, and love. You might also note the feelings you would like to have accompany these emotions, which might include peace, contentment and focus.

2. Write down activities that give you the experience of being closest to the emotions you want.

Barriers to Your Inner Peace

Our culture often focuses on how peace can be had by accumulating things. A common practice when people are feeling down is to buy something. Other people fill their schedule with activities, while others have a constant barrage of stimuli. It seems that many people have the TV going while multi-tasking several text messages at once. Although we are all different and people can find these activities fulfilling, they can also be the very actions that take away from our inner peace.

For example - One time I had dinner at one of these places that re-enacts medieval battles (don't judge) and bought a large glass and small banner with the logo on it. When I got the glass and banner home I did not know what to do with it. I eventually put it on top of my bookshelf and it just seemed to clutter things up. The point I am trying to make here is that I bought something that I thought would bring me joy, but instead was just cluttering my house. It was too much stimuli for me to take into my living space and I did not need it. I was just accumulating too much and it was filling in too much of my living space.

How many times have I heard mothers talk about their schedules? I do not know how they do it. They take their kids to a sporting practice after school, dance classes, tae kwon do, scouts, birthday parties, clubs, music lessons etc. The week and weekend schedule are jammed with activities and yet you are not really spending any time with your family, other than being a chauffeur. Life has no area for you to breathe. Mothers often don't allow areas in their lives in which to breathe, or for their families to breathe.

While most people are spending their lives trying to fill it up with things to find peace, it is my observation people come by peace through making space in their live to allow a certain flow to begin.
Here are some examples of what you can reduce in your life to increase the flow.

Fear

We are all born with a certain something that we are meant to bring to this planet. This certain something is in your heart. In your natural relaxed state, it is obvious to you. The goal of this book is to keep you in that natural state so you can continuously feel your heart's desire. In order to keep your heart's desire burning brightly you must take steps that bring you closer to protecting your inner peace. One of the biggest obstacles to people taking those steps forward is fear.

If you think about what keeps you from doing what you really want to do for your career, then you immediately start thinking about the fears of not making money and not having benefits, and the impact these things have on your family. Think about how fear for the security and safety of your future keep you from venturing out toward your bigger dreams. You start thinking about the start up costs and the time it would cut into your already busy schedule. You may think about your current unfulfilling job.

These fears are what cover up that burning desire you keep in your heart. The goal of this book is to teach you to protect yourself from these fears that cover your heart. This would include thoughts, work, obligations and people that cover up what you are really feeling in your heart. These are what I will be addressing.

When I was in graduate school, I was extremely busy. I was working full time and taking classes when I was not working. When somebody asked me what I wanted to do when

I had free time coming up or what I wanted for my birthday, my mind would go blank; I couldn't describe what I wanted. There were so many obligations covering me that I could not think of what I truly wanted. As anyone nears their graduation they are plagued with the question of what they want to do. Again, the obligations make this very difficult to see. As time went on my obligations became smaller and I researched various goals that allowed my fears to subside; I had something that was unique for me to offer others.

I had a message that I wanted to get out to the world based on all of the things that I kept hearing in my counseling sessions with others. I found when I said certain statements and asked certain questions people began to feel better. I wanted to write these things in a book, but I had too many fears about the book not being published. The fears included not finding a publisher, people not buying the book, people criticizing my writings or thinking I really did not know what I was talking about.

Toxic People
Often times a manipulative person will seek out the really good person who has a strong sense of obligation and is afraid of conflict. They will pretend to be offended or they will be very charismatic in getting you to do things that are really their responsibility. They are masters at making you feel like it is your obligation. Again, the key here is not changing the other people, but changing how you "block" people like this. Dealing with this kind of person is what much of the later chapters of this book will be addressing.

You are Overreacting

Many times people are simply stuck in their own world and do not realize the hurt they may be causing. Many times we can add a negative meaning into very neutral actions of others or we may put a negative meaning on an intended positive action of others.

An example of this might be a man who comes home and always checks the mail first. His wife gets upset and offended at the fact that he gets the mail first. She goes to a place in her mind that the mail is more important to him than she is and that is why he gets the mail first. The wife overreacts and scolds him for his selfishness for checking the mail when she does so much for him. Her husband gets offended and the couple gets into an argument that distances them from each other and takes away from their inner peace. Later, the husband explains that he gets the mail because he wants to get the last business of the day over with so he can focus on her. Not only is the wife hurt from his counter attacks, but now she also feels bad about all of these wrong assumptions she has made about him. It was her meaning that she put onto the situation that caused her pain, not the action or attitude of her husband. We will be discussing this phenomenon in greater detail in "The Mirror" portion of the book.

Drift

This is the sneakiest of reasons why you lose your inner peace and thus lose sight of your heart's desire. These are the things you allow to happen to yourself that are circumstantial; free time that you have which mysteriously disappears before your eyes.

See if this sounds familiar. You come back from running an errand and you discover you have some alone time without obligations for a solid block of two hours. You are musing about all the things you could choose to do with that block of time. You may want to take that much needed nap. You might want to read that great novel or gossip magazine. You may be thinking of doing yoga or meditation. It may just be that you don't want to make any decisions and let mindlessness fill up your time. Your blissful state is interrupted by the sight of the package of meat that was left on the counter top. You grab the package to return it to the refrigerator and you answer the ringing phone. When you went to answer the phone, the package of meat tipped in such a way it dripped juice on the floor. You efficiently put the package on a plate, which you put into the fridge, while writing down the phone number from the recorded message about some billing issue. You are now spending your time returning the call you missed, plodding your way through menus and talking with someone you can barely understand about a billing issue that is probably not your fault but the fault of a big company. By the time you wade through all of this and clean up the meat juice, your blissful peace is shattered. You have continued the hamster wheel of life. You have perpetuated the belief that if you are not running constantly, you are falling behind. Your free time has drifted away from you. Later chapters will be addressing ways to set boundaries around time for yourself.

Anger

Many times we try to mask our weaker emotions of hurt, fear

and helplessness with anger. If not properly channeled anger can be a source of violence and destruction. We will be discussing how to cope with anger later in the book. Anger often leads to revenge and other actions that take away from our inner peace. It is important that we explore what is behind our anger so we can become more peaceful within our interactions with others.

Remember the Main Themes of this Book

- Ways to protect your true self in your peaceful state.

- Taking responsibility for the things that happen to you is a liberating experience.

- Keeping your mind clear and focused on your objectives.

- Learning how principles of peace can be effective even during conflict.

- Learning Eastern and Western ideas from all ages that help you develop a strong peace by connecting you with your highest self so you do not feel the need to protect yourself.

Making Peace with Warriors

Warriors have committed some of the most deplorable acts in history. There are accounts of burning cities needlessly, violating holy grounds, vandalizing artistic masterpieces, destroying architectural marvels, torture, terrorism, forcing people to give up their deepest religious beliefs to replace them with those of the conquering warrior and raping women and children. It is no wonder warriors get such a bad rap. Make no mistake; there have been people like this in every point in history up through the present day. I am not asking that you justify these behaviors. These behaviors are unacceptable and not the spirit of the true warrior, for the last thing a true warrior wants is war.

A true warrior is one who protects others by taking care of themselves. A true warrior is interested in self-mastery. The greatest warriors throughout history gave us visions of how they protected peace within themselves so they could build a society and keep it safe from being attacked. True warriors are compassionate, protective and merciful. A true warrior wants to stay safe with the minimum amount of harm to anyone. They realize that on some level we are all connected to each other and to hurt another is ultimately hurting ourselves.

The "Warriors" or Martial Artists I Know

Ironically, most of the martial artists I know personally; e.g., my kung fu teacher, my Aikido Senseis and students who are veterans from actual wars, are actually very nice people. Many people make the mistake of stereotyping martial artists as competitive bullies flaunting their fighting prowess. I have seen people like this for sure, but the people who incorporate this training as a lifestyle have a completely different philosophy. They tend to be healers and artists. They tend to be very concerned about the welfare of women and children as well as the state of the world as a whole. These attitudes are demonstrated through their actions and choice of careers.

The martial artists I know practice self-control and, in most cases, never use their martial arts skills. They are very different from the people who use or study martial arts for the wrong reasons.

Famous Martial Artists You May Know
Bruce Lee had a whole philosophy about life and martial arts. Chuck Norris is a devout Christian who developed a martial art based on the philosophy of "Universal Way" called Chun Kuk Do. Steven Seagal is a devout Buddhist who prays every morning and does charity work with children. This is not what one might expect from people who have the skill to kick someone's butt. Compassion is an underlying theme with many of those who are truly trained in the spirit of true martial arts.

Historical Warriors Show Compassion

The "Dark Ages" received its name partially because of the brutality of what happened during those times. If we look at some of the more famous warriors who came out of that era then we begin to find that they had some sort of nurturing quality that was part of their code.

- Knights Templar provided protection and medical care for travelers. They set up banking systems that served as a basis for our modern day banking. They also offered protection, guidance and healing to those traveling to the holy lands.

- Knights Hospitaller had the word hospital in their title for the care they provided to pilgrims in the holy lands

- Merovingian Kings have legends of having healing powers and the ability to talk with animals. The Merovingian history has a controversial lineage.

- Knights of the Round Table were said to be protectors of the weak and the just. Legend reports that King Arthur was able to unite Great Britain through peaceful means of negotiation and trade.

Peace is Even Effective in War

As the industrial revolution progressed individuals and nations began to realize that there were better means of getting what you want. Trade and commerce were the way people were getting their needs met. This part of history produced some individuals who learned that peace was a more effective way of getting things done, even in times of war. Often times they were not even warriors, but peaceful people who made their groups, armies and nations stronger by using peaceful means.

Florence Nightingale was an English nurse who was one clear example of a peaceful person who helped to strengthen the army she treated. She pioneered the nursing field by emphasizing proper hygiene in her treatment of soldiers and measuring statistical outcomes with her mathematical skills. As a result of her work in the mid 1850's soldier mortality rates dropped from 42.7 percent to 2.2 percent. This extremely lowered rate was not some new military strategy. It was the peaceful act of healing that created a stronger army. Obviously an army that is going to lose 2.2 percent of its wounded population is going to be stronger than the one that loses 42.7 percent of its population.

In 1859, the Swiss businessman Henri Dunant arrived in Solferino, Italy, where the Battle of Solferino and San Martino was being waged the day of his arrival. While he did not witness the battle, he took a tour of the battlefield later. Dunant observed thirty-eight thousand soldiers lying on the battlefield, dead, dying or wounded. He took it upon himself to organize a civilian force to set up shelter and provide treatment for the soldiers on both sides of the conflict, with an "All Are Brothers" attitude, thus starting the International Red Cross, in 1864, which also led to the creation of the Geneva Convention. Even though Dunant could not stop the war he did take steps to make it more humane.

World War I Assessments, Examples of Compassion by the Military, 1917.

When the US military made assessments of all of the men who were considered for the armed forces during World War I, they found something alarming. Military assessments revealed half of the men evaluated for service fit the label of being "feeble minded." We do not really know what that term actually means, since we have many more sophisticated ways to describe feeble mindedness today, but the crisis created an upsurge of improvements in the way they handled mental health assessments. The mental health of individuals was finally getting attention in the industrial age. People were receiving treatment that used new and effective psychological techniques we still use today. This new psychological treatment led to people feeling better and being more productive. These treatments would not have come to light if it were not for these new military assessments based on compassion. Although not all people were treatable, there were a great number of people who were transformed into productive citizens after a short period of treatment.

Connecting with Others is Effective

An Air Force officer under the pseudonym of Matthew Alexander writes that compassion, rapport, flattery and deception are the keys to obtaining information from the world's most dangerous terrorists.

It seems counter-intuitive that being nice to a terrorist would be the right thing to do. If you want to get information that could save the lives of thousands, it seems that connecting is an effective approach even in an interrogation-style setting during a war.

Nation Building Effort

Nation building is when the United States puts money toward countries we have recently invaded. The movement is an effort to gain allies and assist in stabilizing the country with the goal that, ultimately, the US will gain enhanced actions through commerce. Looking at nation building efforts it appears there are more peaceful activities than harming activities.

Coming Full Circle

Most of us are born with the feeling there is something more meaningful within us and therefore something more to life than where we are presently. We feel that our daily jobs are just a fraction of what we are capable of doing. There is something that touches the core of who we are. That something within us knows that anything is possible, even though our daily setbacks cloud our vision of what once was clear to us as children. For example, as children we knew we were connected with the rest of the universe. We could be happy just because it was a clear day and we felt good.

The objective of this book is to address these issues through a combination of scientific research, intuition and what I have observed in working with people throughout my career that I never learned from books.

A Martial Arts Metaphor for Peace

To best way to illustrate how to protect your inner peace is ironically, to use a martial arts metaphor. There is a whole spiritual aspect that goes along with martial arts. Just as you could take a yoga class and get the physical benefits of the physical exercise, there is also a deeper spiritual element that could be explored that becomes a meaningful way of life. You could study yoga with a master in an ashram (traditional yoga school) and receive the richness that can enhance your life in more ways than you could imagine. The same is true in martial arts. It is a spiritual guide that can apply in any situation. You don't have to abandon your spiritual beliefs. The desired outcome is that this way of life will help enrich your understanding and following of your current beliefs. Even if you do not believe in God or you are devout in your own religion, I hope this new way of thinking will take you to a higher place that leads to a more fulfilling life and greater inner peace.

5 Strategies for Protecting Your Inner Peace.

1. Sorting it all out

2. Protecting yourself

3. Making sure you are heard

4. Forming alliances

5. Seeing things as they are

Sorting it All Out

One of the best ways to figure out how to "sort it all out" is by doing the following exercise.

1. Write out a list of at least 20 things getting in the way of your fulfillment. These can be as severe as the death of a loved one or as minor as what you read in the tabloids. Think of all the mundane chores, all the way to the big hurts. Think about the closets that need to be cleaned out, funding your retirement, paying for your kid's college, cleaning the car, registering your appliances, what happens when you are not around your kids, taxes, getting rid of things in the basement/attic, your significant

other, extended family, friends, neighbors, your job and your weight. If nothing else comes to mind, then think about things that you have complained about within the last month and put them on your list.

Here is what a typical list might look like.

A. Betrayal of a close friend.
B. Break up from six months ago
C. Needing to organize the garage
D. The latest celebrity news about who cheated on who
E. Health care reform
F. How my co-worker dresses
G. Death of a relative 3 years ago.
H. A neighbor who is making more work for himself by not listening to my suggestions.
I. Laundry
J. Wasting time finding things in a disorganized house.
K. Critical family member.
L. Errands
M. Your car is not working so well
N. Co-worker not doing their share
O. Getting upset with the environmental situation

2. Stand up and hold your arms out at shoulder height then twist at the waist. If you were looking at yourself from up

above, what shape would you be making with your arms? (Hint: It's round.)

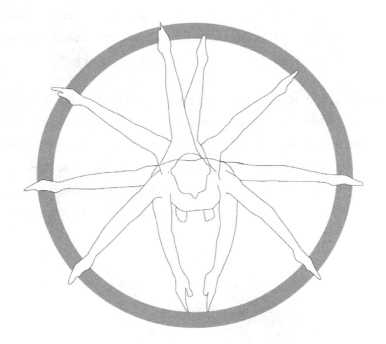

3. Draw a large circle that fills a piece of paper to represent the area that lies within your arms' reach.

4. Think about if there is some benefit to taking on the problems on your list and write it on the circle in the following way: If it is a core issue put it in the center of the circle; If it is something that would benefit you to address and heal, then put it where you think it belongs in your circle. An example of this would be if someone close to you recently died; then it would be important for you to address the pain

that goes along with this so you don't have to carry it. You would write this issue in the center of your circle, because it is probably impacting you to the core. If you recently had a tooth filled and it is still a little sore from a few days ago, then you might put that at the edge of the circle.

5. If it is something that you are taking on that you don't need to address—e. g., getting mad with fictional characters, getting angry with the latest celebrity news or a neighbor wearing outdated clothes—then you would write these issues outside of the circle. A loss that happened a long time ago, but still affects you from time to time, would be more on the edge of the circle.

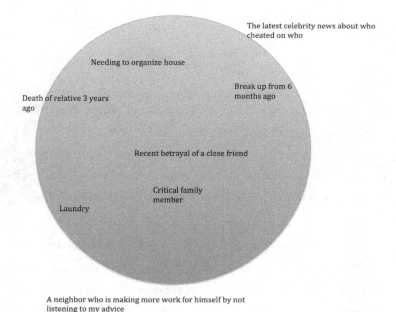

22 | PROTECTING YOUR INNER PEACE

When you map out your stressors it might look like the above diagram. There are some things that affect your emotional core and need some time for healing. There are some things that you do not have to take on at all because they are outside of your circle. The things that you have control of releasing are burdens you can let go of completely to have a greater amount of energy to focus on the things that really matter inside of your circle.

One woman shared in a workshop that she would argue with the people at home who criticized the people on television. She realized, after being confronted, that she was wasting a lot of energy in defending the people on the television, because the people on the television did not impact her circle. The people on the television would probably not be impacted by what the people in her living room were saying about them.

Think about what the implications of your circle map is telling you.

Here are some things that have come up in workshops.

1. There are things that I have been worrying about that don't impact my space at all.
2. I put more emphasis on things outside of my circle that don't impact me and less energy on the things that would actually change my life.
3. I never realized how much something affects me.
4. It's easier to get caught up in the drama outside of my circle than to deal with my issues.

SORTING IT ALL OUT | 23

The two conclusions most people have drawn from this activity are:

1. They can be most effective by focusing on taking responsibility for what happens in their personal space.

2. This is the only space over which we have any control.

The Wisdom to Know the Difference

A western version of this eastern concept is the Serenity prayer.

The Serenity Prayer

God grant me the serenity
to accept the things I cannot change;
courage to change the things I can;
and wisdom to know the difference…

— Reinhold Niebuhr

An eastern form of mental health therapy is called Morita Therapy, which is summarized in the following quote:

"In Morita Therapy, character is developed by cultivating mindfulness, knowing what is controllable and what is not controllable, and seeing what is so without attachment to expectations. Knowing what one is doing, knowing what the situation is requiring, and knowing the relationship between the two are quintessential to self-validation, effective living, and personal fulfillment."

— Shoma Morita, M.D.

My First Master Teacher - Liu Siong - Willem Reeders

When I was 5 years old I took classes from my teacher's teacher, Master Liu Siong. He received the title of Grand Master of Kung Fu from a group of martial arts practitioners and was known worldwide for his skill. He was even consulted for the Kung Fu series that was loosely based on Liu Siong's experiences training in a Shao Lin Temple. The temple is a holy place and is a traditional setting for meditation, spiritual discipline and martial arts training, the way it was intended to be passed on to students. Liu Siong's conditioning was not like the training of more modern martial artists. He learned the old way martial arts had been taught over thousands of years. Liu Siong passed on his wisdom to his top student, with whom I have studied martial arts for over ten years; in traditional teaching, wisdom is the ultimate goal of martial arts. At sixteen, I was happy to merely make it through high school alive, being the skinny honor student that I was. I learned that in Liu Siong's view, the ultimate goal of martial arts was to heal. I never really understood what he meant by martial arts leading to healing until I began taking Aikido and expanding my mental health work in crisis intervention.

Liu Siong was adept at many forms of martial arts, including Aikido. After more than ten years studying kung fu under Liu Siong's top student, I went on expanding my career as a mental health therapist. I found the philosophies between good mental health and what I learned in martial arts classes so similar that I had to start writing down my thoughts about it.

This led me to start taking classes in Aikido, which is sometimes called the Art of Peace.

Morihei Ueshiba-O'Sensei

In the 20th century a new form of martial arts emerged from another man who studied a variety of martial arts. The story goes that Morihei Ueshiba, better known as O'Sensei, was challenged by a swordsman to fight. The swordsman attacked O'Sensei repeatedly, to the point of exhaustion. O'Sensei moved out of the way of every attack, did not counter attack and remained unscathed. The swordsman was too tired to continue his attacks and walked away from the challenge with nothing harmed other than his ego.

Immediately after the conflict it was said that O'Sensei was surrounded in a golden mist that came with visions of a higher consciousness and world peace. This inspiration led Ueshiba to develop a peaceful martial art form that was strictly defensive with the goal of turning violent situations into peaceful outcomes.

What is Aikido?

It is a spiritual practice that works in harmony with your life force, called ki, as in Aikido/Reiki or chi in Chinese, as in tai chi. It is strictly designed as a defensive art with no initial attacking moves in its form. It uses a person's own force against him with the goal of rendering your opponent defenseless with the least amount of harm done to him. The techniques are usually rounded and involve moving out of the way of a force coming at the defender so that the attacker has nothing to push up against.

What is the Space Inside Our Personal Circle and How does this Tie into Aikido?

The Circle, of course, represents the radius of space we can reach with our hands and feet. This space is your inner peace. It is your personal sphere of influence, where you can cause change and create the life that you want. It is where you play, decide, and manifest your successes.

This is the only area over which we have any kind of influence. We cannot have any influence over our world unless we change what happens inside this circle. If we want to straighten a picture that is across the room, then we have to move our feet, which are within the circle, to move us over to the picture. Then we can use our hands to make the adjustments.

In martial arts people have learned to extend their circles by using weapons. But you can expand the circle only a few feet. However, there are other tools that can have a greater influence on the world instead of weapons. We can pick up the phone or get on the internet to order something, which sets off a whole chain of events that lead to something being delivered to your door. Now the influence of your circle has expanded across the globe.

The external world can be altered with our hands and our feet can take us to where we want to go.

Everything starts with a thought. Our thoughts eventually lead to physical manifestations that we can see on the planet.

If you have an idea about your house being a different color, then you go to the paint store and look at the variety of colors. You select a color and paint it or hire someone else to paint it. On a grander scale, many of the world's holy books have inspired people to build churches, temples, and monuments throughout the world.

Even the swordsman knew that the pen was mightier than the sword. Writing your thoughts can not only extend your reach farther than a few feet, but can expand your influence over time. Sharing thoughts can cause some of the greatest manifestations or changes. Writing something can also influence others, well beyond a person's reach. If you write something down, then your words have the potential to have an impact on anyone on the planet and to be viewed at any time from this day forth. Something as simple as a one-page document of the Declaration of Independence has resounded throughout the world since the day of its inception.

There are many famous warriors who wrote books in an attempt to influence others. One of the most influential was the Roman Emperor Marcus Aurelius whose memoirs from over 1800 years ago are still quoted today.

Other examples are two famous samurai, named Tesshu and Musashi. Tesshu wrote about his enlightened understanding of "No Sword" during 1800s when he realized that there is no enemy, but only perfect form.

Musashi wrote The Book of Five Rings. This book has influenced people for almost 400 years. The book is used in business today.

We cannot make people do things, but we can change how we react to things. As a result of our changes we can be more persuasive and people will be more likely to change.

Journaling has been found to be an effective way to bring inner peace to a person with regular practice.

The Border of the Circle

The border of our personal circle or space is a cup-like vessel that holds our essence, energy, dreams and emotions, which I compare to the properties of water. The area within the borders of the cup is also your inner peace.

This space is viewed differently by different people. If you are more of an atheist or if you just put more emphasis on scientific reasoning, then this space has more to do with having more free time, less stress and psychological freedom. More traditional religions would view this space as God's divine power running through you. Christians might say it is grace.

East Indian culture believes there is a tube that extends from the top of your head to the base of your spine, if you are sitting, or to your feet, if you are standing. The belief, as it is practiced in Yoga, is that this tube contains an energy called prana and the Yoga movements help to maximize this prana flow.

As mentioned earlier in the Chinese culture, there is a similar force that runs the length of your body called "chi" (pronounced chee) as in Tai-Chi. In Japan, this force is called "ki" (pronounced key) as in Ai-"Ki"-do.

The energy held within your circle is your ki force. The water within the cup serves you best when it is calm, because the surface of the water accurately reflects your surroundings when it is flat. I will discuss how to do this throughout the following chapters.

All of us have a personal circle of space, but some people are more aware of their circles than others. There are ways we can expand our circle and ways to release the burdens of our circle.

Throughout these writings, I will discuss various aspects of the circle. I will discuss how people will try to shove their responsibilities into your circle and what you can do to address the situation as quickly as possible. This will be done by either defending your circle, so you can stop others before they cross the line, or by avoiding the situation altogether.

The circle also works like the cross section of a tube that delivers the chi (life force). As your issues, obligations and self-sabotage collect on the inside walls of this pipe, the opening that allows your chi/life force to move is constricted and narrows the free flow of energy. Sometimes the pipe is narrowed because you cannot say **"no"** to other people out of fear of conflict.

The Backpack

The space within the circle is also a representation of a metaphorical backpack that holds all of the responsibilities that you carry in everyday life. Throughout the day people try to put their responsibilities into your backpack to lighten their own load. This makes your load more burdensome. Someone leaves out the dirty dishes. It is everyone's responsibility to either wash their own dishes or put them in the dishwasher. Now that the dirty dishes are left out someone else's burden from their backpack is now placed into your backpack. If you leave the dirty dishes for the other person then you have sanitation or convenience issues that will burden them.

We all have a sense of this obligation. We feel a sense of obligation to the people we love, like our aging parents or children. We feel the burden when we have a financial debt. We feel the burden when we have hurt someone's feelings or have not done our share of the work on a task. We feel the obligation weighing us down and even have the expression of **'having a monkey on our back.'**

This emotional backpack is up to us to own. If I drop something on the floor, it is up to me to pick it up. It does not matter how much money I make or what my status is. The responsibility of picking up something I dropped is still mine.

The same is true with our mental health issues. We all have emotional injuries from our past that we carry with us. It is up to us to manage these in a respectful way when interacting with others. If someone close to you died and you are still deeply wounded by this, it is completely understandable that such a tragedy would stay with you. But it would be up to you to own and manage that tragedy. If someone made a joke around Halloween about dead people, then you may end up feeling bad inside, even though Halloween is filled with images of zombies and the like. It would not be okay for you to verbally punish the person for being insensitive. It is not okay for an obsessive-compulsive person to demand that all people who prepare his food wear gloves. These are issues that each individual will have to find ways of coping with to meet their own emotional needs.

If an alcoholic, who is in recovery, goes to a social gathering, it is his responsibility to remove himself from the situation if he gets too tempted to drink. It is unreasonable to ask other people not to drink in that kind of a social situation.

We all have stuff to manage in our emotional backpack. When we don't deal with our emotional "baggage" we are often told to "lighten up" as part of the solution. The hard truth to face is that we are responsible for everything that happens within the circle. We are responsible for what our outcomes are and we have to live with the outcomes of the decisions we make. If we face the issues that we have, then we can be fulfilled. If we ignore the truths about ourselves, then we are victims of the circumstances that surprise us.

Our Circle is our personal space with a perimeter barrier that should not be crossed unless we invite someone to enter. The circumference of the circle is the very line that is "drawn in the sand" where all non-peaceful energies must stop. It serves as an armor or guardian that protects all that we hold most dear. This is the boundary you maintain. This is what we are talking about when we say, "you are stepping on my toes." Most of us know how to stand up to the annoying salesman who pushes you to just have a few moments of your time. Most of us say "no." That issue becomes much more challenging when it is a loved one whose feelings we care about or some kind of client who is somehow one of your sources of income. Sometimes it is a person with greater power than you, such as a boss or some other authority figure. Then saying "no" becomes much more difficult, because these are people you have to maintain a connection with. At the same time you cannot keep depleting your resources by allowing draining people to take from you. The circle is your border that keeps the requests and obligations from stripping away your free time. This book will be addressing the more challenging situations that arise with people we care about.

The border of the circle is the protection of our private thoughts and the gatekeeper of the information we choose to release. Just as we do not want harmful forces entering our circle, we do not want valuable/private information leaking out of our borders. I am not only talking about your social security number and your mother's maiden name. I am also talking about information that could potentially keep you excluded from certain circles and keep you from growth opportunities. Sometimes expressing your cutting edge views during an interview or sharing intense emotional subjects with people you have just met can scare away people and the opportunities that come with them. Often times men need to keep vulnerable emotions to themselves when they are with other men out of fear of being criticized by other men. They are often called babies, wimps or worse. Sharing your views on politics and religion is also risky. It can create a fast friend or shut you out of opportunities. Discussions about religion can create a firestorm of emotions, as well. So this aspect of your circle monitors all of the information you let out of your borders.

Addictions

Sometimes the pipe is closed due to addictions to drugs or alcohol. There is a lot of time spent wondering when the next fix will come. For instance, will there be alcohol at the restaurant tonight? A smoker will obsess about the spontaneous evening ahead, because they will not know if they will be able to gracefully exit a social situation. They do not know if there is going to be a place where they can inconspicuously smoke without violating someone's space. They may have to go the entire time without smoking.

Hidden Addictions

Many people find comfort that they do not have addictions since they do not use drugs or alcohol. Most of the time our pipes narrow because we take our sights off our big goals and fill our time with TV, Facebook, internet surfing, computer games, etc. All of these activities are fine and can provide a refuge from reality, but often times they are fillers that help us procrastinate our true mission. There is a big difference between watching a good movie on TV versus channel surfing to fill the time.

Our life force gets covered up with stressors, obligations and impurities. As more of your circle gets covered up, you can become more sluggish, depressed and tired. Sometimes people have so much of their circle covered they forget who they are. If someone asked you what you wanted for your birthday, would you be able to answer him or her? If you had a week off to yourself, would you know where you would want to go or what you would want to do?

Some religions refer to these barriers to your life force as **"sins."** It is the impurities of life that suffocate your life force making it more difficult for you to manifest your dreams and create inner peace. Sometimes these barriers are created with the intent of doing good things. We volunteer for the project that we do not really want to do. We end up in a conversation that makes us late for our deadlines or we spend more on an item, because we are afraid to negotiate a lower price.

As the layers collect on the surface of this pipe they can slow the flow of life to a sluggish pace called depression or squeeze it up to a racing anxiety. While you are juggling ten balls in the air, your boss may ask you to do something well within your job description. You then become very tense because you are so layered up with other obligations restricting your flow. We have an intuitive sense of this in our common phrases. We talk about being smothered.

This squeeze or suffocation can manifest itself in your body physically. In the short term, your blood vessels constrict which cause a racing of blood that creates a condition called stress. On a long-term basis we can create a condition of adding exterior layers of fat to our bodies that cause us to be sluggish called obesity. Other physical manifestations are the layers that line the inside of our blood vessels, which can eventually lead to heart attack, stroke or some other disease.

When we completely block ourselves up completely with these layers emotionally, we create a condition called a crisis.

We will be addressing ways to keep these layers to a minimum or transform them into enjoyable moments.

Benefits of the Peaceful Life

More Effectiveness and Less Drama

Neighborhoods can have their share of drama with people being overly concerned about how other people are conducting their lives. People judge their neighbors for the clothes they wear or the habits they have. If a habit includes being noisy, then that habit does impact your space, but many times their habits do not impact your space. It may be the neighbor checks the mailbox often or other strange quirks that do not impact your space at all.

Many times in the various work situations I have experienced I will encounter people who are always trying to track just how much other people are doing. Most of the time people get it wrong and have no idea how to track other co-workers. Often times the people who makes the biggest show about all that they are doing gets all of the credit. These co-workers inquire about how much a person might be making. The gossip is so passionate sometimes that you would think that people earned a commission based on catching other people not working. It is almost as if these hall monitors want to catch a person not working and get some of their salary. I am not talking about situations where co-workers truly put a burden on you by not holding up their end. I am talking about people who work in completely different departments who have no influence on the other person whatsoever. The reality of the situation is most of the time gossipers are talking about people and behaviors that have absolutely no impact on their circle at all.

The irony is these gossipy people are not being effective in their jobs when they are so involved in the lives of others. When people focus on their own inner peace, not only are they doing the job they are supposed to be doing, they are also steering their current situation toward more fulfilling goals for themselves. In cultivating their inner peace they are making the world a better place for everyone without bringing harm to others.

Reduces Judgment to the Degree it Impacts Your Circle for Couples

One thing people do, particularly couples, is when there is a disagreement about something they waste a lot of energy trying to prove to the other person they are a better person or they are **"right."** One person will put the other down in an attempt to show they are more balanced or their way is better. What happens is people don't end up addressing what really needs to be addressed.

We will use the example of a married couple to illustrate this. The man wants to watch something comical on TV and his wife wants to watch a movie based on the true story of a woman's personal trials. They cannot come to any agreement, so they start arguing. The wife starts to make the case that the comedy is silly and immature. The husband counters with how ridiculous it is to watch a sappy, depressing movie. Each is hurting the other's feelings by putting each other down while not expressing what they really want. If one person wants to watch a comedy and the other person wants to watch a Lifetime movie, then it does not have to impact anyone's space. But when both people want to watch a movie together, that does impact each of their personal spaces. When people focus on what impacts their space it leads to more fulfilling lives. In this example, the couple could pick from thousands of movies that are available to them. There is bound to be a movie that both people would like watching together. Maybe the issue is not the movie at all. Maybe it is spending time together.

Greater Peace/Piece of Mind. (Opinions)

If someone has a different opinion from you it does not have to impact your circle. What gets confusing is that a lot of times opinions fuel what behaviors people choose and that can impact your space, thus infringing on your inner peace. So let's take a look at someone you work with. He or she starts spewing their religious views at you, knowing you disagree with them. You start addressing the ridiculousness of their claims. You suddenly discover you are in another argument that has you riled up to the point you cannot think. This is an attack on your inner peace and you let it happen to yourself. You cannot control what other people think. You certainly will not change the opinions of this other person, but there are some things you can do to protect your inner peace.

Instead of trying to change the other person's opinion you could focus on changing the person's behaviors by confronting the real issue.

Religious Antogonist: Did you hear what happened with how your church messed up the world this time?

You: I would like to have a good working relationship with you. You know we have different opinions that lead to us arguing and I would like to have friendlier conversations with you. I would appreciate you keeping your religious views to yourself.

Notice the goal of the interaction. We often fool ourselves into thinking the goal of our interactions is to change everyone else's opinion so we can have peace. In the example given, you are protecting your peace by managing the other person's actions, because chances are the actions will be easier to change than the person's opinion.

Marcus Aurelius
Let opinion be taken away, and no man will think himself wronged. If no man shall think himself wronged, then is there no more any such thing as wrong. (trans. Meric Casaubon)

Stress management research has finally caught up with the wisdom of what the Roman Emperor knew almost two thousand years ago. It is not the stressor that interrupts our inner peace as much as how we react to the stressor that impacts us.

PART 2
PROTECTING YOURSELF FROM OTHERS

Blocks & Evading

In martial arts, when a kick or a strike comes toward you, you have three options that you have in that circumstance. The first option is to let yourself be struck. Not a very good option, but we live in a free will universe. The second option is to get out of the way. This is a better option, but we don't always have the luxury of having enough time to move quickly enough. When this happens we sometimes have the third option of blocking available to us. A block in martial arts is when you either stop or redirect an attack from your opponent that was intended to harm you. Many times martial artists use their forearms to block kicks and strikes. When hand-held weapons block someone it is often referred to as a parry, as when one swordsman stops another's sword with his own sword.

Blocks in Everyday Life
As most of us know, most of our attacks happen off of the battlefield in our everyday life. The definition of a block is slightly different when used in this sense and is defined as follows:

A defense against unwanted tasks, obligations or a reduction of resources of value. In other words, something that protects your inner peace.

Prevention
Having systems in place for defense, before the worst happens, is the best defense of all. Keeping unwanted forces from entering the circle is easier than removing them once they have entered. Developing a system for prevention is your best defense.

Blocking Techniques
In martial arts blocking techniques are usually a hand or forearm guiding the incoming strike away from more vulnerable parts within the circle. In non-combat situations, a block is a shield from issues that slow your progress toward your heart's desires. These issues are labeled as "strikes." Sometimes strikes come from other people or the strike is a life circumstance. A housemate or family member leaving dirty dishes for you is a strike against you by another person. Having to delay your plans due to weather or to address a physical need are circumstantial strikes.

Evade, Align, Enter
Evade, align and enter are the basic steps in Aikido that allow

you to defend yourself under the most difficult combat situations. Using this technique to protect yourself in real-life verbal situation can be very effective as well.

Evade - When someone approaches you in a tirade with lots of emotional energy behind it, and does not allow you to speak, then the best approach is to evade. That means verbally getting out of the way until the energy is dissipated.

Align - After the energy has dissipated, then it is your opportunity to align with the person by first validating their concerns. We will be talking more about validation in the next chapter, but basically you start out with agreeing with the part of your opponent's statement that is true.

Enter - Once you have engaged the other person through aligning with them, then you have an opportunity to enter their space with the message you want to deliver when it is actually being heard. This is what we refer to in the next chapter as a strike.

Blocking a Smaller Opponent

A smaller opponent is a person who has less leverage over you than you have over your opponent. The power shift can be constant or change from situation to situation. When a smaller opponent attacks you in a fight you can hold out your hand and stop the strike cold. In a non-combat situation, you can tell others "no" when they try to place unnecessary obligations onto your circle. When the power difference is big enough, stopping the strike can be done with little negative consequence to the more powerful contender.

Salesman: Let me take just a moment of your time to show you all of the fabulous...

You: No, thank you.

This short response ends the interaction without negative consequences to you.

Blocking a Larger Opponent

Stopping a smaller opponent is easy. When your opponent is larger than you and running toward you at top speed, stopping the superior force coming at you is not an option. Putting up your hands to stop your opponent would only result in the opponent bowling you over on your back. The technique of yielding and overcoming would be needed to overcome this opponent. Stepping out of the way and throwing your opponent in the same direction as his run would likely be a more effective technique. The same is true in a non-combative situation. When you have someone with superior leverage over you, it is difficult to succeed, long term, by sheer refusal. In an earlier example, a boss imposes inappropriate expectations on his employee. Using the yield and overcome approach would first mean agreeing to the demands of your boss and fulfilling them, because you need your job. Second, you would look for other work or find leverage within the organization to help remedy the problem.

Blocking an Equal Opponent

Someone of equal leverage requires more adaptability because the powers shift more often. You might have the ability to drive in big cities, but your peer might have more knowledge of the current city in which you are driving. In this circumstance, the power could shift moment to moment and your response to strikes would have to change as quickly.

Personal Policy

One of the best defenses is to have a series of protective personal policies set up to shield you from things that you do not want in your life. This is a great way to get clear in your mind about how far you will allow others to come into your circle, if at all.

One useful personal policy, when you are selling something, is to keep in mind the lowest price that you will take for the product. The lowest price you decide is expressed as your personal policy. I will not accept anything less than _____ for the car. You can reinforce your personal policy by preparing reasons to convince yourself that this is the best move. When selling a car, the reasons may include: the great condition of the car, the fact that you have all the repair receipts, and that the price is the same as the market Blue Book value of other cars of the same make and model.

Another personal policy might be that you refuse to answer your phone after 9PM or that you will not purchase anything over the phone. Nothing stops a con artist better than saying, "I don't buy anything over a hundred dollars without getting a second opinion."

Here are some other common policies that have proved successful for others:

- I don't have more than two drinks during an evening out.

- I keep to myself what others say to me.
- I don't lend money to people outside of my family.
- I insist upon a credit report before I rent to someone.

The Attack: Someone tries to grab your arm that mirrors your arm (e.g., opponent grabbing your left hand with his/her right hand).

Aikido Move:

- Open your left hand with your fingers fully extended, and make a "C" shape with your hand.
- Rotate your left arm clockwise so your opponent's wrist is able to fit in the "C" shape of your hand.
- Push your opponent's wrist directly across your opponent's body until they release your hand.

Aikido Intention: Keep your opponent out of your space by peacefully defending your boundary by escaping a hold.

Interpersonal Intention: Peacefully keep someone from "holding" you to an obligation that does not belong to you.

The next two interpersonal techniques are an example of how a personal policy might look.

The Bus Leaves at 6:30

This is a great defense to use when you offer to give people a ride. You need to put the responsibility inside the other person's circle, where it belongs. You say, "I am leaving at 6:30. If you are here at that time, I'll be happy to take you with me." That way, you're not in a position where you are calling people and saying, "Are you coming?" You can leave on time, guilt free, knowing that you set up clear expectations. There is no room for doubt as to what is going to happen if your friends don't meet you on time. This will work much better than saying, " You're always late! How can you be so rude — making me wait for you all of the time?"

How this technique looks while adding the Aikido techniques of Evade, Align and Enter:

Evade: There is nothing really to evade here since you already want to take your friend with you on your terms.

Align: I would really like you to come with me and I would be happy to take you along.

Enter: It is very important to me that I leave by 6:30 and I will have to leave exactly at that time, even if you are not ready.

We Have Ten Dollars for the Day

This technique is similar to the bus technique and is particularly helpful in situations involving older children. Instead of subjecting yourself to a barrage of begging, you set the limits of your circle up front. When you are at the fair, inform each child that they will be given ten dollars for the day. When your kids start begging, you can say, "I'll be happy to get that for you, but you'll only have five dollars left for the entire day."

If you are getting inundated with requests for favors, a token system can work. You give your child three tokens at the beginning of the day. You insist on getting a token before you do a favor. When the tokens are used up, hold out your hand for a token. When your child says he used up his tokens, lovingly remind him that he will need to wait until he has a new set of tokens tomorrow.

Evade: Letting the kids ask for favors or money.

Align: I am happy to help you out/get things for you.

Enter: There is a limit to what I can do for you.

Monkey in the Middle

While stocking shelves in a retail store, a manager asked me to arrange the inventory on the shelves with items to the front of the shelf. Another day, a different manager asked that I push the items back on the shelf. Both managers had logical reasons for their preferences on shelf management, but I was the monkey in the middle. I would spend one day undoing what I had finished the day before. One day, both managers were together and one had asked me to stock the shelves in his particular style. I took the opportunity to ask both of them to work out an agreement. The burden of undoing my work from the previous day was now off of me and placed on the two managers to decide. They came to an agreement about different rules for different items.

The Attack: Two people try to pull you in two different directions by tugging on each of your arms.

Aikido Move: Shiho nage

Twist your body as you make this move and grab your opponent's wrist with your left hand.

Extend your opponent's wrist enough to take him off balance while taking a step.

After that, keep you feet planted and twist the upper body as you make a sword cut over your right shoulder with the opponent's wrist.

Aikido Intention: Bring both opponents together (and away from you) when they are tugging on you in opposite directions.

Interpersonal Intention: Get two people together who have different agendas for you and have them work out the differences that really exist between them.

Evade: Letting the two bosses tell you opposite directives and going along with it to keep peace with each boss.

Align: I want to be a good employee by doing the right thing and follow your directives…

Enter: I am getting confused about each boss telling me an opposite directive. Is there a way that you could work this out with the other boss?

Example: Caught between your spouse and adult child with conflicting agendas about how you will spend your time.

Evade: Listening to the requests of both your spouse and your adult child.

Align: I really want to participate with you…

Enter: I also have plans at that same time with (adult child/spouse). Why don't we all get on the phone and see if there is any flexibility to work out a solution to this?

Get Out of the Crossfire!

This is very much like monkey in the middle. Person A complains to you about person B. Person B complains to you about person A. Person A, all of the sudden, wants to know what person B is saying to you and vice versa. The result of offering opinions and breaking confidentialities is that both people get upset with you. The best thing to do is to turn this communication triangle into a straight line. With each person firing complaints and inquiries at you like arrows, you need get out of the crossfire. Let each party know that the other person has important issues to discuss with him or her directly. Set limits about what you will hear or what you will say. Communicate how both parties are creating a difficult situation for you.

The Attack: Two people are attacking while one attacker has grabbed your left wrist. The other opponent is moving in to attack you.

Aikido Move: Kaiten nage

Step toward your left, to the right side of your grabbing attacker, while avoiding the oncoming attacker.

As you step, extend your left arm straight as you make a clockwise circle that cuts downward.

This will straighten out your grabbing opponent's arm as you crank the arm behind your opponent with your left hand, propelling him into the oncoming opponent, you will be pulling his upper body downward and using it as a guiding hand.

Aikido Intention: Get away from the attacker who is holding you while escaping a second attacker who is moving in to hit you from another direction.

Interpersonal Intention: Get out of the way and out of the conflict that really exists between two other people who are trying to get you involved.

Example: Each family member urges you to tell him or her what the other is saying about him or her. The question each member asks is "What did they say?"

Evade: Letting each family member complain about the other family member.

Align: I really want you to know that I stand by you and I want you to know that when you tell me something I don't repeat it to anyone else.

Enter: I'm sure you'll understand why I don't want to tell you what they said.

Pick Your Battles

The best way to prevent getting hurt from an attack is to minimize the number of battles you choose. It is true that when people know that you will not fight back they are more likely to attack you. It is also true that you have nothing to defend if a total stranger insults you. It could escalate into something dangerous, if you chose to argue with them.

At home, we need to evaluate what affects our space and what is simply our ego trying to "fix" others.

Let's say you and your spouse each have your own medicine cabinet. You see your spouse reach into their own cabinet and pull out their own razor and it is in a spot that really does not make sense to you. After observing this, you make a comment how your spouse should put the razor in a different location. Your spouse says that they know to get the razor from that location, because they have been doing it that way for years. You push the issue in the name of "helping" your spouse, even though you do not see the inside of the medicine cabinet and you do not need any of its contents. This issue does not have to impact your space. If you let the issue go, then it would not matter how your spouse arranges their medicine cabinet.

Strikes

To injure an opponent is to injure yourself. To control aggression without inflicting injury is the Art of Peace. –O'Sensei

Growing up in a Christian faith there is the concept of one bread one body. It essentially says we are all one, so the idea of hurting someone else means we are actually hurting ourselves. When we discuss "strikes" in this section we are actually talking about something that is very powerful and helpful.

I define strikes in the following way:

Making a statement or request that gets past a person's defenses so that the message is actually heard by the targeted person with the accuracy of the spirit it was intended. What I mean by this an effective strike really means you accurately receive the message I am trying to convey to you without your wall going up or defenses getting in the way of my message.

Scrutinize before the Strike

About twenty years ago I was moving into an apartment and was setting up the utilities. I made it very clear to the power company I wanted to have the power turned on before I moved in and specified an exact date. I called the day before to verify the situation and the power company reassured me I would have electricity when I moved into the apartment.

The next day when I moved in, I tried to turn on the lights and nothing happened. I went to change the thermostat and nothing happened. I was fuming at this point. I had to go across the street to use a pay-phone (remember this was a few years ago) to call the power company. I had a flash of wisdom and thought I better ask a few questions before I exploded on the person answering the phone. I explained my situation and asked about what was keeping me from having power in my apartment. The employee calmly explained the power was turned on and I started to gear up for the big blast of a fight. The person on the phone rapidly deflated my intentions when she asked if I had switched on the circuit breaker. Oops! Imagine how foolish I would have felt if I went for the jugular and screamed at the worker. This is why it is important to scrutinize the situation.

Before we can deliver a difficult message, it is important to scrutinize. Many times, if we do research and exploration, the very issues we think we need to express to other people to improve our situation are the very things we need to hear ourselves. In other words, before we try communicating a message to other people, we may want to consider if the situation we are trying to resolve might be our mistake.

There are times when you do want to get your point across to another person and there are steps you can take that can be more effective in getting them to listen. When we talk about the "strike" portion of this book, we are talking about the Evade and Entering steps mentioned earlier. You will want to align yourself with your opponent to set up for the entering Strike.

Ask Questions. (Do you want to be Understood?)
Asking questions not only helps you to scrutinize the situation, it also helps to settle your mind. Asking questions provides the advantages of making sure the situation is as you understand it to be, or helping you figure out if it is something different. It also helps you to understand the other person, which can often lead to the revelation they are not an opponent at all.

Snake Past the Head Games (Tenshinage Irimi)
Many times in my career, I would be drawing something on a dry erase board and the child I was working with would try to grab the pen from me. I had the option of either trying to yank the pen from the child's hand, which led to a fun contest with the child continuing with the bad behavior. Scolding the child often leads to the child becoming rebellious. What I have found to be effective is snaking past the head games. What I mean by that is telling people what behavior you want from

them; this is often the most effective method. In this case, I had a lot of success by telling the children, "Let go of the pen."

Let's apply this technique to a more complex situation. Every time a certain person sees you, he tries to impose their political views on you while knowing their views are different from yours. You have made it clear several times you do not agree with this person about their politics. Many of us get drawn into the trap of trying to change the opinions of others. We discussed earlier how we are wasting our energy, trying to change the opinions of others, and a different opinion is not something that impacts our personal space. The actions that are motivated by the different opinion impact our space. In this case, the different opinion politically motivates the other person to violate your space with their unwanted views.

The other issue is many of us have the delusion that we will change the opinions of others. Many of us carry this myth that if only we could get it through the thick heads of others, that we, not they, are the rational ones. When they see we are more balanced, they may finally see the light, and the situation will be resolved.

So what do you do with this situation? You snake past the head games; e.g., "Stop talking about politics around me." This is a clear and rational directive to change their behavior.

The Attack: Someone grabs your mirror hand; e.g, opponent grabs your right hand with their left hand.

Aikido Move: Tenshinage - irimi

Sprawl the fingers of your right hand open and make an "S" shape with the path of your hand.

Start with moving your hand to the center of your opponent's body, then moving your hand to the left side of your opponent's head.

Aikido Intention: Get out of the trap by moving your hand directly past a person's head.

Interpersonal Intention: Go past the trap of arguing with someone's head games onto directly asking for your needs.

Example: A person with a different political view tries to get you to change your mind OR your spouse argues about which TV show is better to watch.

Evade: Let the other person state their opinion and see if it stops on its own.

Align: I really want to have a good working relationship with you and get along with you very well.

Enter: It is difficult for me to get along with you when you discuss politics with me. I would appreciate it if you would stop.

Wait Them Out (Karate Kid)

One of the most educational jobs I've had was at a National Call Center for a Fortune 100 Company where all the crisis calls were funneled to the department in which I worked. At least a few times a week I would receive a call where someone would talk constantly for a full five minutes. I found myself trying to squeeze in a word, but could not. My end of the conversation looked something like this:

"Well...If you...Something you...There's a..."

I would hear my co-worker yell out, "Ma'am, I'm only trying to help!" I would get frustrated and stressed about these calls until one day I had a revelation. I realized that I did not have to say anything. I could just wait them out.

I sat there listening to these phone calls as each person blasted away and steam-rolled over everything that I was about to say. I relaxed and let the conversations happen. Many times they asked me multiple questions without giving me time to answer. At some point in the conversation the other person realized I was not saying anything. It was only at this point was I able to enter and strike. I would often ask, "Which one of those ten questions would you like me to answer?" I might also instruct the person that I am not going to speak until they are ready to listen.

The Attack: Your opponent tries to draw you in by expending a lot of energy, but not quite entering your circle.

Aikido Move: Maintain visual contact with your opponent to maintain safety as you wait for your opponent's energy to diminish as he remains outside the range of your circle. If your opponent enters your circle at a later time, then you align and enter according to your opponents attack with your opponent's energy diminished.

Evade: While the person is expending a lot of energy outside of your circle and out of harm's way, watch vigilantly that the person does not enter the circle, and wait for them to wear themselves out. When your opponent shows signs of fatigue and falters, then you enter to diffuse the attack.

Align: I really want to help you and want you to know that you are heard.

Enter: What can we do for a next step?

Aikido Intention: Stay out of harm's way until your opponent is worn out, gives up or leaves.

Interpersonal Intention: Prevent yourself from stepping into a verbal attack when the person is full of energy and wait until they have expended their energy before trying to reason with them.

Expose the Inconsistency (Ryotedori Irimi)

There is a martial arts move that can be done when someone grabs onto our two hands and tries to hold them. It involves moving both hands in opposite directions and splitting the other person open. The move is effective, because it is very difficult for people to maintain a position that is going in two different directions. The same situation is true in a social situation.

Many times we hear people say these blanket statements:

I'll always be there for you.
My door is never closed.
Whatever you need...
We will do everything by the book.

What happens often times is when the day-to-day struggles emerge and the time to step up to these idealistic statements arises, the other person does not follow through on those ideals. This is an opportunity to remind people of the discrepancy between the ideals and the actions the person is presenting in the here and now. In a sense you are splitting the person apart (in a gentle, compassionate kind of way) to expose which way the person will be going.

In the above examples it might look like this:

I'll always be there for you. – (Align) You often say that you will always be there for me, but (Enter) I have called several times to get some help from you and you have not responded. What's going on?

My door is never closed. - (Align) Your door has been open when I have tried to get up with you several times to have a discussion with you (enter) and you never seem to have the time. That seems inconsistent with "my door is never closed" approach. Is everything ok?

The other person often yields to their more idealistic statement and you can get the desired result. If the person does not yield, then it at least reveals to you and others you are dealing with a person of bad character. This kind of realization can replace feelings of insecurity with a sense of peace.

The Attack: Someone grabs both of your arms while pushing you backwards.

Aikido Move: (High - Low Ryototori irimi)

Take your left arm up by your opponent's ear and take your right arm down by your opponent's knee.

Slide your right leg in the backward direction so that your opponent is pushing back on your right side as you sink down.

Aikido Intention: Overcome your opponent by spreading his arms (and energy) in two completely different directions, thus taking him off balance.

Interpersonal Intention: Expose the differences between the high ideal promises someone makes and the actual behaviors/decisions one actually exhibits, thus taking him off balance.

Example: A salesman presents lofty ideas about his customer service, but refuses to remedy the mistakes he made on your purchase.

Evade: Give the salesman an opportunity to make corrections on the mistake.

Align: I get that you don't want people cheating you out of money.

Enter: I also need to know if you are going to stand on your promise of good customer service or if you are going to show me that you really don't mean that by not helping me.

Pre-Emptive Strike on Repeated Attacks. (Morning Phone Calls)

In Aikido there are no attacking moves, because the focus is on defending yourself without hurting the other person. There are times when it is appropriate to make a statement to someone else in a proactive way when you see a pattern developing that takes away from your resources. Here are two examples:

1. A family member calls you several days in a row to tell you about a crisis just before you have to go to work.

2. A client calls you a couple of weeks in a row at five minutes before closing. He is aware of your closing time, but continues to call you at that time. You are not able to help, because the other resources you need to resolve the problem have left for the weekend.

In the first example a pre-emptive strike might look like this:

Wake up early enough to address the issues with your family member. Give them an early call as you explain the reason for your call. Explain you wanted to make sure you could give your family member the time and attention they deserve to resolve the conflict. This puts the responsibility back on the person to resolve the issues that are happening in their lives. It gives you the opportunity to genuinely help your relative and strengthen your relationship with them. If your relative is not having a genuine crisis, then they will likely not appreciate your response to their early morning calls and will likely stop their early morning calls to you. If you think that calling early in the morning is too risky for disrupting the peace in your relationship, then you may want to call the person the day before the expected crisis. Either way you get a more peaceful outcome to the situation.

Aikido Intention: Enter into your opponent's attack with a disarming move before he can attack again.

Interpersonal Intention: Address the situation proactively, when a person makes more than one attack, before the other person tries to take away resources from you again.

Evade: Letting the situation happen until you detect a pattern.

Aligning: I really want to help you with your problem.

Entering: I called you earlier so I could be more effective at helping you prevent your crisis from erupting. What can I do to help you prevent a crisis?

Exercise:
How could you apply this technique to the second example?

If I was Your Favorite Brother, Uncle, Sister... (Cradle Irimi)

Exactly one month after I was married, I saw my wife placed in the back of an ambulance and taken to a major hospital suffering from intense headaches. After her hospital stay, we spoke with several specialists who basically had the same answer but were not able to help us. Finally, I asked the doctor this question.

"If I was your brother and this was your sister-in-law having these headaches, what next step would you have her take?"

The doctor stopped for a moment deep in thought. I interpreted the doctor to be going through a transformation, from the position of seeing my wife as just another patient on a long list of patients, to seeing her as a real human being. The doctor exclaimed with a wide-eyed, **"OH"** and explained that he was only there to tell her the very best news he could give her: that he did not have to operate on her brain. He then offered his professional advice to see a neurologist. We were able to resolve the issue.

This is an effective way to help people refocus and think about your situation in a different light. Make sure that you emphasize their advice is off the record. You will not hold them responsible.

The Attack: Someone tries to backhand you to keep you away by sweeping their right arm toward your face.

Aikido Move: Irimi nage

Bring your arm to meet your opponent's right arm in a blending motion as you step in to have your arm and body align with your opponent's body.

Your chest should be near your opponent's back and your right arm should be inside your opponent's right arm.

Place your opponent's head on your right shoulder as your right arm and right leg circle back 180 degrees.

Step in with your right foot as your right arm circles in front of your opponent's neck with your hand going over your opponent's left shoulder.

Aikido Intention: Enter and bring an opponent who is trying to keep you at bay with a sweeping backhand attack closer to you.

Interpersonal Intention: Get closer to someone who is trying to keep you at bay by not disclosing the information you need; this is done by asking them to imagine you as a family member and requesting that they guide you to the next step.

Example: If I was your brother/sister...What is my next step?

Evade: Allow the other person enough time to see if they will eventually hear your message.

If they don't hear your message, then move to the next step.

Align: You know a lot more about this than I do.

Enter: If I was your brother what would you tell me to do for my next step.

Go Straight for the Emotions

This technique could be used for many occasions, but it is particularly effective when someone dances on the outside boundaries of your circle. You know the type of people who roll their eyes at you or say comments in a cutting way, while denying the intended meaning. There can be many times when we make wrong assumptions about people's behaviors, but there are times when there is a history of repeated events **where** there can be more reason to believe something passive-aggressive is going on.

So what do you do when this happens with someone and it is beginning to impact your space? You can ask the question "is there something wrong?" You can state you have reason to suspect the other person has some strong emotions toward you and discuss the behaviors as evidence.

"I notice when I am around you, you sigh and roll your eyes a lot. Although you deny there is anything wrong, I am getting the sense you have some strong feelings about me. I'd like to know what those emotions are about."

Emotions are at the very core of issues between how people interact with each other, even when it is in a professional setting. Confronting people with the core issues of emotions usually ends up with one of two results:

Either people run away for fear of dealing with their emotions or they yield to your request and start discussing the real issues behind the conflict.

The Attack: Someone grabs your opposite hand — e.g., right hand to right hand — and they will not let go.

Aikido Move: One-handed Nikyo

Stretch open the fingers of your right hand.

Bring the fingers of your right hand over the top of your opponent's wrist in a clockwise motion.

Point your index and middle finger toward the center of your opponent's body as you push in that direction.

Aikido Intention: Escape an attacker's hold by pointing directly toward a person's core (center of the body).

Interpersonal Intention: Get a person to yield to your point or leave you alone when you are focusing on the core emotions that are involved in a passive aggressive conflict.

Example: What to do about passive aggressive behaviors — confront opponent with emotions of mad, sad, glad, scared or shame.

Evade: Allow enough events to happen so that you have a good basis for your suspicion of passive aggressive behaviors.

Align: It seems like you have some strong emotions about this and I would like to hear what you have to say.

Enter: Tell me about the emotions you are feeling toward me.

Yield and Overcome (Picking Up the Penny)

Let's say you are leading a meeting for a community organization and you attempt to present a variety of solutions to a problem the group is experiencing. As you are presenting the solutions there is someone in your group who chimes in with negative comments about your ideas not working. The person is loud and gladly presents reasons why your idea will not work.

You could try to tell the person to stop talking, since they are challenging your authority, but that would likely create a conflict while showing others you do not value the input of others.

The likely outcome the person interrupting you is trying to achieve is to challenge your authority. When someone challenges your authority you can yield and overcome. This is done by offering the heckler an opportunity to take the lead.

You: It seems you have some strong ideas about what we should do here. (Aligning)

Heckler: I don't think any of your ideas will work.

You: If you have any ideas on what will work, then we would be happy to hear them. (Entering)

At this point, if the heckler has a constructive idea then it would be valuable to listen and use their ideas; everybody would benefit. Most likely, the heckler is trying to give you a hard time and will likely stop his behavior.

The Attack: A person attacks you with superior force; e.g., swinging a baseball bat at you with their right hand.

Aikido Move: (picking up the penny)

As your opponent swings the bat with his right hand from his outside to hit you on your left side, you spin into his inside and grab his right wrist with your right hand.

After you grab the right wrist you should be facing in the same direction as your opponent (aligning).

Drop your weight as you pull their wrist downward.

Aikido Intention: Overcome your opponent with superior force by taking him off balance by putting yourself in the lower position.

Interpersonal Intention: Overcome a person with superior force by allowing them to have their faulty way and have them fail.

Example: A blowhard dominates your conversation and criticizes your ideas in a group.

Evade: You let a comment go by to see if it was an isolated incident.

Align: It sounds like you have some good ideas that would be helpful to everyone.

Enter: Why don't you share your ideas with everyone.

By surrendering and giving the blowhard the attention that he wants, you are able to strengthen your authority. If you told him to be quiet then he would be able to resist you by saying no to you.

Natural Consequences

A friend of mine requested a bigger workspace from his boss several times over a two-year period because of safety concerns over a cramped work area. My friend sent several memos to his boss, none of which were ever addressed. Eventually, an accident occurred in which someone suffered a permanent injury, as was foreseen by my friend. His boss sent a memo, asking my friend how something like this could happen. My friend stapled copies of the memos he had previously sent to his boss's memo and returned the stack of memos to him. Eventually a budget was granted for a larger work area.

The Attack: Someone tries to strangle you.

Aikido Move: Nikyo
Grab your opponent's right hand with your right hand. Pull your opponent's fingers up toward the ceiling and toward your opponent.

Use your left hand to bend your opponent's arm in a "Z" type of pattern.

Aikido Intention: Overcome your opponent by turning his own fingers against him until he yields.

Interpersonal Intention: Use the factual information about your opponent's faulty ideas against him until he yields to the new ideas, which need to be considered.

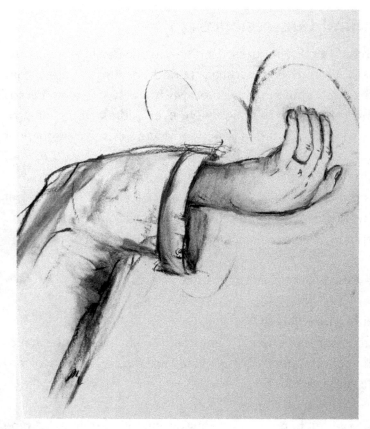

Example: A boss makes you use an idea you know has failed many times in the past. He begins to blame you when the idea fails once again.

Evade: Follow through with your boss' request, even though you know that it will likely fail.

Align: Let your boss know that you respect his/her authority and that you are not looking to rebel against it.

Enter: Attempt to let your boss know the potential negative outcomes of his directive. If he does not listen, document and objectively measure the outcomes of your boss' directive while noting your suggestions to your boss. When the outcome becomes evident — that your boss' directives are not working — then you can show your boss and others the documentation. This may take time before the outcome is evident.

Exercise
- Have one person use **Strikes** to get your partner to volunteer for your agency.
- Have the other person use **Blocks** to keep from volunteering.

PART 3
Alliances

One of my favorite activities in my workshops is to have people challenge each other to an arm wrestling competition. The challenge is if you get your opponent's arm to touch the ground you get an M&M. If they touch your arm to the ground, then they get the candy. Usually I see people struggle as they try to get their opponent's arm to the ground. Some people try a more defensive approach and focus on keeping their arm from hitting the ground. I have seen so many people struggle and strain, just to get a few morsels of candy. It is quite entertaining to watch. All of this hard work continues and yet it is so unnecessary.

One problem that happens is people associate winning or achieving their goal with beating the other person. If the goal is to get more candy then beating the other person is not what you want to do. The most effective way to get the most candy is to let the other person win with the agreement they will let you win. The people who use this technique get far more candy than the people who are even a lot stronger than everybody else, because everybody is working toward a common goal without resistance. This is the essence of the advantages of alliances. Two people working together toward a common goal is much more effective and enjoyable than competing. Unhealthy competition can bring the disadvantages of sabotage and hurt feelings.

In Aikido there is a relationship between you and the person who is attacking you in practice. If you see two people throwing each other around in an Aikido demonstration there is a good chance they like and trust each other very much. This seems strange when you watch two people going at it. You would think they dislike each other very much. The relationship exists with an understanding that the attacker (nage) safely prepares the defender (uke) for real life combat within the skill level of the defender. The defender safely averts the attack within the skill level of the attacker's ability to fall and roll. This makes for a bond that exists and becomes a fluid circle of energy. There is a state of bliss that occurs when this flow is uninterrupted and the techniques begin to happen without thinking about how you are going to do them.

Relationships – Forming Alliances

Relationships are very important for our well being. Up to this point we have discussed the most important relationship of all and that is your relationship with yourself. The methods described previously can help you to keep safe as you challenge your comfort zone, but let's focus next on relationships with others. There is nothing you can do or tell me that would convince me that relationships are unimportant. In every discipline relationships are the magic ingredient that determines success or failure.

Examples:
1. Customers buy a product after multiple contacts with the salesperson. The stronger the relationship the more likely the sale.

2. In the field of mental health the most important factor in successfully reaching treatment goals is the relationship with the therapist.

3. The better the relationship with the teacher, the more likely the students will learn.

4. The better the relationship with the health practitioner, the less likely the patient will sue for malpractice.

5. Ask any lawyer about the importance of having a good relationship with a jury.

6. Companies have learned the better they treat their employees the more work they can get from them, for less money.

7. If you want a quality life, nurture quality relationships.

Advantages & Disadvantages

No matter how advanced you are or how strong you are, you are never as strong as the person who is positively connected with a large network of friends who are willing to help them out. This universal truth is true in modern social life as well as in a martial arts situation. In addition to providing you assistance directly, allies can provide you with the latest news, information and resources that can put you ahead of any one strong individual trying to make it on their own. The size of the force of people who are able to help you can be the key to reaching whatever goal it is that you are trying to reach. When talking about allies I mean friends, acquaintances, contacts and like-minded people on the same team as you at various levels of personal and professional contact. I am talking about people who are willing to help you get to the next step of where you want to be. There are many levels to this alliance. Obviously, the guy who sold you the pack of gum is not going to be at the same level of ally/friendship as your life-long friend.

The disadvantages of forming alliances with other people is that in order for an alliance to work, there has to be some level of allowing people into more vulnerable parts of yourself. Each person you take into your life has the potential to harm you with each step they take past your defenses. This is not often the case, but it is possible.

Each life decision brings in its own element of risk. If you do not have allies then you do not have access to the emotional support, resources and networking with others and that can compromise your peace of mind **and** quality of life greatly. If you allow people to get close to you then you run the risk of getting burned. The solution to this is to develop skills that minimize your risk while still allowing you to connect with others.

How do I connect with others? Validate!

What is Validation?

Rather than give you a definition, let's take a look at my adaptation of Aesop's Sun and Wind Fable.

One day the Wind challenged the Sun in a contest to see who could get the coat off the man they saw walking. The Sun agreed to the contest. The Wind blew a strong and forceful blast of cold with a determination to force the coat off of the man. Despite the Wind's best efforts to blow a strong gust, the man only pulled his coat tighter around himself.

The Sun stepped up and took his turn to try and force the man to remove his coat, but tried a different approach. The Sun shone brightly and warmly. The man began to get hot and the only way he could get comfortable was to take off his coat.

The story serves as a perfect metaphor about what validation is and how powerful it can be in getting people to drop their defenses. Through emotional warmth and an attempt to get some level of understanding, you can get others to lower their defenses. The Wind tried to get the man's coat off through force and as a result he strengthened his defenses. The Sun created a climate of warmth and safety. The man could take his coat off without fear of getting cold. We can create a climate of warmth so others lower their defenses and validation is what creates warmth and safety.

(Validation) to Get the Walls to Come Down.

Validation is one of the most powerful skills you can develop in establishing a relationship. Many times people will reveal a lot about themselves just through this one technique alone. This technique is so powerful police interrogators use it to get criminals to make a voluntary confession.

I once had a very powerful experience in a workshop I was conducting where I had one person discuss a problem while the other person gave validating remarks. I intended for the exercise to go five minutes, at which point I informed the group that time was up. The group continued to talk. I prompted the group several times before realizing that I just needed to let them go. The group went on for twenty minutes before I was able to get the group to wind down from the exercise.

For a strike to be effective in the entering process you must get the wall to come down. We have all been in situations where we felt like we were talking to a brick wall. Our instincts are usually correct.

See if this sounds familiar:

WIFE: ...and then she did this and then she did that. I can't believe how hard she is trying to get me.

HUSBAND: I'm sure you are just over reacting. She's not trying to get you. She's just upset. What you should do is...

WIFE: OVERREACTING! She's been trying to take me down ever since I met her. What do you call it when she...

Validating, reaffirming or empathizing with a person's feelings is often more effective than trying to minimize them. In the above example a statement about how it must be rough to be around someone who is trying to get you could be stated first. If you try to problem-solve or say that the person is misreading the situation it will only keep the wall up. Continue to console the person with statements that help the person identify their feelings first. Once the person understands you are on their side and want to hear their feelings, only then does the wall come down. Only after the wall comes down can you effectively engage with the other person's circle and attempt to direct them.

Example
WIFE: She did this and she did that...

HUSBAND: Wow, she's been doing a lot of things that upset you. (Validating and aligning)

WIFE: Not only that, she made this comment with such a sarcastic tone and then just stared at me.

HUSBAND: I would probably feel uncomfortable with that. (Validating and aligning)

WIFE: That's exactly how I felt. (This is when the wall has come down and you can enter)

HUSBAND: You can't live the rest of your life like this. You are obviously unhappy. What are you going to do?

WIFE: I don't know.

HUSBAND: Is it possible that she doesn't realize how sarcastic she sounds? (This is very different than saying, "She probably doesn't realize how sarcastic she sounds." This is probably what you might want to say initially, but resist the temptation. Don't enter when the wall is up.)

Alliance Exercise:

The next time someone comes to you with an issue they are having, try using words of validation to support the other person. Note if the other person's responses change.

Validating words you could use may include:

I never realized how much you were going through.

How do you stay sane in that situation?

I am so sorry that you went through all of that.

You deserve better than that.

You probably feel pretty bad about that don't you?

Getting to Know Others

We may live within a circle, but we do not live on an island. There are times when it can be advantageous to allow someone inside our circle. Provided that a person passes the scrutiny of the questions in the proceeding paragraphs , you can benefit in many ways from allowing people within the outer levels of your circle. This overlapping of circles can enhance your space by providing more information, resources, and support than you could ever achieve on your own. When people join forces they can consolidate experiences within a short period of time. Sometimes these experiences add to your circle and sometimes they are detrimental. When they diminish your circle it is time to let the person go or attempt to fix the problem. When a person adds to your circle you can strengthen the bonds and reach deeper levels of trust. Two individuals can strengthen their trust in each other by passing tests during times of adversity. When we see others perform during difficult times, we can allow them more access to the more vulnerable parts of our being. We start off with minor risks and move deeper. When we move to the deeper levels of trust we gain the advantages of people doing more for us and building forces. Armies are built with people who have overcome adversities together and have seen people demonstrate their character under pressure. You can build your army by friendliness (getting the walls to drop in others), and by rewarding the deeds people perform for you. To get people to drop their guards and trust you, there is one technique that is more effective than others. It is recognizing that there are levels of information and being very mindful when you enter deeper levels of communication.

Here are the levels of communication within your circle.

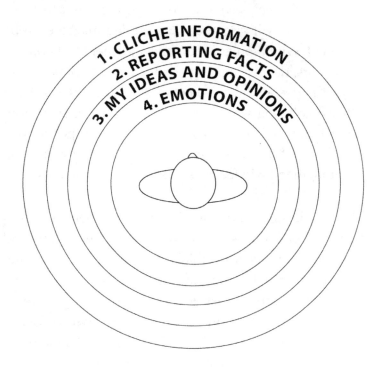

1. The outer edge of the circle is cliché conversation. It is very safe to discuss the weather or wish someone a nice day, even if you have never met them.

2. The second level is "Reporting Facts." This involves discussions about what other people are doing. "Did you notice what the temperature was?" OR... "I read salaries will rise ten percent next year in the computer industry."

3. The next deeper level of the circle is "My Ideas and Opinions." When giving an opinion there is a risk the other person will disagree with you and maybe even be offended. When someone voices a judgment that concurs with yours, deeper trust is gained. Differing opinions also establish deeper trust. Sometimes individuals test each other by offering an opinion that might be different from other individuals only to see how the other person will handle it. "If the other person is okay with my differing opinion, then I will feel safe to share more opinions."

4. The next level is emotions. The difference between emotions and opinions is emotions disclose how we feel and opinions show what we think. If you share with another that snakes frighten you, an individual could approach you with a rubber snake to find pleasure in your reaction. A person who truly cares about you will go out of their way to protect you from seeing snakes. So there is a greater risk as well as greater possible gain.

Emotional discussions need to include some form of the words mad, sad, glad, scared or ashamed. Other people who are in touch with their emotions tend to get closer to those who share their emotions. There are some people you will find who, when you share your emotions, think of you as weak and you run the risk of having people view you in that way if you share with the wrong person. If you share with the right person, who respects your feelings, then the strength of your relationship can survive anything. It is possible to share your most private thoughts.

The final level is full self-disclosure. A childhood trauma or a very personal situation shared with another is the greatest area of risk and gain. Discussing your antidepressants, abuse as a child, bad credit rating, or your childhood police record could either open yourself up to ridicule or nourish a lifelong friendship. This is about as close to the core of the circle as you want another to reach.

Ground zero — it is not necessary for you to share every little part of your life with another, even if you have been married to each other for many years. There are some things you can keep to yourself and don't have any obligation to tell anyone else. A spouse telling the other about the positive aspects of a former lover will not make the marriage a closer one. Complaining about every annoyance that enters your life will not help either. Many times thoughts are not even clear enough to express to others and need to be explored before it is possible to share. Our thoughts are the last freedom that we have and there is no way for anyone to steal your thoughts.

When is it Safe to Let Others In?'

The next part of getting to know others is figuring out when it is safe to let others enter deeper parts of your circle. The safest approach is to see if you can trust people with the outer layers of your circle before trusting them with deeper levels of your circle. Sometimes you can figure this out quickly and sometimes it takes a while for you to figure it out. Sometimes you have to rely on your intuition, but if your intuition is not correct, then at least you have only let them in one step too far. You do not want to delve into deep self-disclosure until a person has proven to you that they can be trusted.

Let's go through the various levels to show you how this would work. If you see a complete stranger while you are waiting a long time to get your hair cut, then you might strike up a conversation with them. You might say, "Hi, how are you doing?" The person looks over at you, as if to acknowledge your icebreaker, then looks away. Maybe they roll their eyes or turn away from you. What has happened is that you have taken a risk that has not worked. You took the first step in getting to know someone and they do not show further interest in getting to know you better so you know it is probably not a good idea to go to deeper levels of conversation.

Let's just say the person says, "I am doing great. How are you doing?" At this point you can continue to talk about the weather and superficial items until you feel more comfortable to move to the next step.

The next step would be to discuss facts. It is easy to find out harmless facts about people and some people might be very cautious about letting you know too much too soon. People are most likely to share what part of town they live in, but do not want to share their address with a complete stranger. Most people are comfortable discussing their profession, but maybe not their specific employer. They might tell you the score of a sporting event or they might report something that happened in the news. If they do not give you information or argue about the facts, then it is a likely that sharing your opinions would not be safe on your part. The responses would be very vague or the person changes the subject. In extreme cases some people may even argue the facts with you. This is a huge red flag for you. Often times abusive people and addicts will argue facts to avoid the truth about themselves. A man might say that he did not tell you to shut up, even though you heard it seconds earlier. An addict might argue that they only had two drinks, when you saw more like ten drinks consumed. Allowing people deep into your circle can be dangerous, if they are not respecting the outer layers of your circle.

Most people will likely respect the facts portion of the circle, but the step from facts to opinions is a bigger step than from cliché remarks to facts. Think about how you feel when you hear these questions:

Where do you see yourself politically?

Do you believe in evolution or creationism?

What are your thoughts on abortion?

What are your views on Jesus?

If a total stranger asked you about these subjects then you may feel a little uncomfortable. Even if your convictions are strong, you may feel you may be getting into an argument with someone or turn someone off. It is okay if people have different opinions from others. There are no two people alike.

It is important though that the opinions are respected. If the other person starts telling you how stupid your opinions are or starts talking over you with their opinions, then it is likely that they will not respect your feelings. However, if the person can differ with you, let you speak, and is genuinely interested in your opinions, despite their differences, then you can safely go to the next level when you are ready.

The feeling level presents a whole new set of risks, by allowing people the most access to what is going on deeply within you. At this level you have the potential to be deeply hurt.

Think about how you would feel if someone asked these questions:

> What was the most hurtful thing that ever happened to you?
>
> When did you feel the most helpless?
>
> Under what circumstances do you cry?
>
> What is the most traumatic thing you have ever experienced?

Imagine a man going up to his marine buddies and talking about how his feelings got hurt. There would be a strong chance he would never be able to live this down. People can learn your weaknesses and use them against you in this way. On the positive side, your emotions can power a relationship that will extend into the rest of your life. When you connect with people on an emotional level then they will be there for you in ways that you never imagined. There is passion that can be present in your life and you can comfortably share your darkest secrets without fear of judgment. You are now linked with someone else as an ally who can be there when you are in the midst of a fight for your inner peace.

Entering Other People's Circles

When entering other people's circles it is important to remember not to go in too fast. Although connecting to someone emotionally is a great goal, with the best of intentions, the very act of getting there too quickly can create the opposite outcome of what you want. What works best in most situations is to spiral through these levels of communication within your circle. The gentle spiral toward the center is a very effective way to get to know someone, while a fast direct path toward a person's emotions will scare someone off, due to the discomfort. Many times people are starving to get their emotions out to a trusted person, and they spill it out before they are ready, and then the trusted person shuts down. When this happens, you can talk about easier topics to address in the outer levels of their circle. You may ask about their next vacation or about how other members of their family are doing to get the conversation going again without delving deeper into the conversation.

Being a Good Friend

In order to have friends, you have to be a good friend. Many people make the mistake of sharing all of their problems with people all of the time. They spill their gloom and doom all over others. When it comes to their friends looking to them for support, then they, all of the sudden, do not have time. Be sure to ask others about how they are doing and what is going on with their families. Empathize with others when they tell you their misfortunes. Offer genuine support and resources when your friends are genuinely in need. Be sure that you pick up on the social cues of people looking at their watches or moving their feet toward the door as they grab the car keys. Revitalize your alliances by offering to have people over. You may have not had good parents who took the time with you to see that your needs were met, but this does not mean that you can expect others to be your parent. In other words, you cannot expect others to just give to you without you giving something back to them. Provide value to your friends and you will have alliances all around you.

Tips for Being a Good Friend

The following sections offer some ideas on how to be a better friend to others. Each section highlights a different quality that will make a person that others will seek out for friendship, because you are giving something of value to others.

Take Responsibility for Your Part

In this next section we will look at two possible ways to respond, both at work and at home. In each of the work/home scenarios there are two options for responding to the situation. One situation will likely add value to you as a friend and ultimately give you more inner peace. The other situation will likely not. See if you can guess which people are more likely to have more peace in their lives.

At Work

The professional who works with you does their job duties, shows up on time, admits mistakes, corrects mistakes and assertively communicates potential problems that may arise.

The slacker works with you, avoids their job duties, shows up late (thus putting some of their work load on your circle), makes excuses/denies/argues about mistakes and gives you no warning about potential problems.

At Home

The friend comes to stay with you for a few days, brings you a gift, picks up after themselves, offers to buy dinner and is respectful of house rules.

The Freeloader comes to stay with you for a few days, expects to be served, does not clean up after themselves and has no regard for your house rules.

If you picked the first person as the person who would have more peace in their life, then you would be like most people. When you take responsibility for yourself you are not a burden to others. When you are not a burden to others there is less potential for conflicts to arise.

We cannot always take care of all of our responsibilities. If you are staying at someone's house and they are at work, then you may not know how to operate the dishwasher or know where the soap is. You can at least pick up your dishes from the table and set them in the sink.

If you are an executive at work and you spill something, then it may not be in the best interest of everyone for you to clean up the spill. You can at least call to delegate the task to the appropriate person.

No one likes to clean up other people's messes and nobody likes it when you do not admit your own fault. Taking responsibility will actually help in keeping your inner peace, because people will have fewer issues with you. When you take care of the business in your circle it does not have to contaminate other people's circles.

Taking the blame for things that go wrong will often facilitate better communication. Unless you are being investigated legally or your employer is exploring how you broke a policy, there is often little consequence for admitting you are wrong. In fact, admitting you are wrong can free up the space with others around you to stop focusing on finding fault and start working on the tasks at hand.

Use "I" Statements

Think about the following statements:

"You hurt me."

"You make me so angry!"

"You are so inconsiderate!"

These statements shift power and responsibility away from you while placing judgment on someone else. You have a choice as to what you feel and often times the person you are accusing does not want to harm you at all. You can never truly claim to read the minds of others. You can know what is in your heart and other people have a harder time manipulating what you know to be true to yourself than what you are trying to guess for others.

So consider the following alternatives to the above statements beginning with "you":

"I got hurt when you_____."

"I get so angry when you _____."

"I don't like it when you _____."

You are taking responsibility for your thoughts and feelings. The other person can either agree with your perceptions of what happened or they can offer an alternative view with you having accused them of doing something wrong. In not accusing others, you are creating a more peaceful environment.

This also works when you want to deliver difficult messages. When someone asks you about a workshop or meeting that was confusing to you, it may be difficult to say how confusing it was. It may be easier to take the blame by saying, "I have a difficult time learning a computer technique without actually seeing it demonstrated on the computer."

Empathize with the Other Person's Circle

How many times have you been driving where you and another driver need to make a turn into the same lane, with equal right of way? You start to move at the same time the other person starts to move. You stop and they stop. You both start again at the same time. If you waved the other person on to go first you would actually take less time than if you tried to figure out who goes first. As soon as you address the other person's needs there is less hassle. In this case, most people want to be first; be clear and be safe.

The more you can put yourself in someone else's shoes the more peace you can have. You are not interested in what a sales person has to offer. But avoiding conflict by suggesting you want to buy while you forward his calls is only going to create more frustration for everyone. Imagine if you were the sales person and someone told you they were interested in your product. You would rather not waste your time with a bad prospect and get a flat "no" so that you could move onto the next person.

Looking at the needs of another person's circle is beneficial to your circle. It helps you to form an alliance with others to bring more resources to the both of you. When you have an alliance with someone you can put your energy toward your goals.

Whenever I have made comments of gratitude or appreciation for someone's craftwork I am always surprised at the extra lengths people will go to give even better service. Life runs a little more smoothly and people give you priority through extra care. Being generous, thoughtful, empathetic, and helpful is one of the most selfish things you can do but pleases everyone around you.

Conflict Resolution: When Circles Collide

Whenever people are near your circle for any length of time there is going to be a conflict. Someone is going to want something of yours or someone will disagree with you about something. There are some important things to remember when you find yourself involved in a conflict.

The problem is what you need to attack — not the person. The object is not to prove the other person wrong, but to work out a solution within their perceptions. Unless you are in a court of law or demonstrating a scientific proof, there is no need to make the other person change their mind. There are often solutions within whatever perception the other person has. Your job is not to change the other person's circle, but to find the best solution within the deeper levels of both circles.

A woman working in a group home overheard two clients arguing over an orange. The woman took the orange and cut it in half and gave each client half of the orange. One client ate half of the orange and threw out the peel. The other client peeled the orange and threw out the orange. It turns out the girl who threw out the orange needed the peel for an ingredient in baking. The staff member cut the orange in half in an attempt to compromise between the needs of the two clients. If the staff member had explored the needs of both people, then both people could have had all of their needs met fully. This is the goal in most conflicts. Unless it violates universal principles, you want both parties to be happy.

Seven Steps to Successfully Manage A Conflict:

Sometimes conflicts cannot be resolved in the simpler steps stated previously. When the conflict is more complex, then it is time to follow the steps outlined below.

Step 1 - Identify Your Problems and Unmet Needs.

You cannot hit a target if you do not know what it is you want to hit. Get clear about what you want. Often times the argument can be resolved just by doing this first step. When you communicate what you want the other person will be more likely to help you meet your needs without having to do the following steps. Before you can communicate what you want you must take care of the business that is solely your responsibility within your circle. You need to decide whether the issue that you want to bring up to the other person is, in fact, a conflict. Many times it is our own misperceptions or the issues may just be a response to an old emotional injury. If this is the case, then it really is not the other person's fault or responsibility to fix and discussing it would cause unnecessary risk of escalating into a conflict.

If you have decided that discussing the issue is something that truly involves the other person and will help create space in your circle that will lead to positive outcomes, then it is important to go onto step 2.

Step 2 - Calmly Describe Your Problems and Needs.

Describe (don't vent) your feelings as well as your ideas. You often get back what you put out in terms of the attitude you use to present your issues. If you present with anger, then you usually get anger back to you. If you present calmly you have a higher chance of a calm response. You may get an angry response despite your calm delivery, but it will not be as negative as if you presented with anger. One of the best ways to do this when you get that queasy feeling in your stomach during a conflict with someone is to use one of the following models:

Quick Fixes to Resolving a Conflict

If the techniques of blocking/evading/aligning-striking/entering are not working then try this next approach. Go back to the outer layers of the circle and discuss the facts of the situation. Once you have clarified what the facts are in the situation, then make it clear to the other person you are discussing your opinions, interpretations or judgments of the situation. These are conclusions you have drawn based on perceptions you have had. These conclusions and perceptions may be very wrong, but they will be a starting point for discussion.

After you have expressed your facts and judgments then allow the other person to either confirm or correct your perception of the situation. You may be surprised at how wrong your perceptions are. You may be thinking that the other person has very negative feelings toward you, when in fact they are ashamed of themselves. Someone may be going through some big issues in their personal life and you are interpreting them to be something against you. This technique allows you to safely explore the conflict.

List the facts about a situation, as you understand them, using I statements.

"I noticed you walked away from me when I asked you a question."

Then discuss your interpretation of these facts.

"I can only think you were acting in a disrespectful way toward me."

Then mention your feelings, if you feel safe enough with the person.

"I feel very hurt when you do this."

Another way to shorten this process is to use the sentence below.

"I feel _____, when you _____. I want _____."

When expressing your "feelings" in a work situation you may want to choose safer words with people you do not trust with your core feelings.

"I feel disrespected when you..." or "I feel insulted when you..." would be some examples of this.

If you are talking to someone you do trust, then you can more safely trust your vulnerable feelings with that person.

The act of doing this helps in many ways. First, the burden within your circle is now placed back on you, thus lowering the chances of defensiveness from the other person. The other person might not do anything for you, but at least you have expressed yourself on the issue and do not have to hold it inside your circle. Make sure you have an end and means in mind.

Many times the conflict will resolve itself by this second step and further steps are not necessary.

Step 3 - Confirm Your Partner's Understanding. Asking Questions can be Helpful.

"Does that make sense to you?"

One of the biggest responsibilities in your circle is taking responsibility for your own communication. Always take the blame and pose it as your inability to express yourself in a way that is understandable.

"Maybe I'm not expressing myself clearly."

Avoid saying, "You don't understand." or "You misunderstood me." Conveying your message clearly is your responsibility. If they do not understand, then you need to clarify.

Step 4 - Solicit Your Partner's Needs.

"What do you want out of this?"

"What can I do differently?"

Step 5 – Check Your Understanding of Your Partner's Needs.

Try paraphrasing; e.g., "If I understand you correctly, you're saying you would like me to include you in these decisions?" or "So what you're saying is..."

As in step 4, if you do not understand what your opponent is saying, then it is your responsibility to say that I do not understand. When you take responsibility for not understanding your opponent is not as likely to get defensive about the discussion and this allows him the opportunity to reword his position.

Understanding your partner is not the same as agreeing with your partner. If you're a woman and a man tells you that men should not have to wash dishes, you can state you acknowledge that the man has a very traditional viewpoint of roles that each gender performs (aligning). This in no way means you agree with it. You are merely getting an accurate view of the other person's perception so you know where you are and what next step to take. In step 6 you can make your point about how you think housework should be distributed, after the man's walls are down (entering).

Step 6 – Negotiate a Solution

1. Identify and define the conflict.

   I want an orange and you want the orange peels for a recipe. There is only one orange available.

2. Generate a number of possible solutions.

   I keep the whole orange for myself.

   You keep the whole orange for yourself.

   I eat the orange and you keep the peel.

   We cut the orange in half and each take half.

3. Decide on the best solution.

   I eat the orange and you keep the peel.

Step 7 – Follow Up the Solution.

After I peel the orange, I will give my opponent the peels.

None of the other steps are worthwhile unless there is follow through on whatever decisions are made.

Step 7 is one of the most challenging steps in the process.

Children and Your Circle

"The martial arts are also the essence of love and the motherly protection of love that love should have."

- Steven Seagal

Most of mainstream psychology agrees that up until age two, the parent is totally responsible for the actions and safety of their children. They are incapable of making good decisions for themselves and need constant supervision. Children at this age are completely inside the circle of your personal game space. As children mature, they become increasingly responsible for their decisions, so part of their circle extends past the perimeter of your circle. A young adult in their early twenties still has some attachment to the parent's circle because young people can still be persuaded by the influence of adults in their lives.

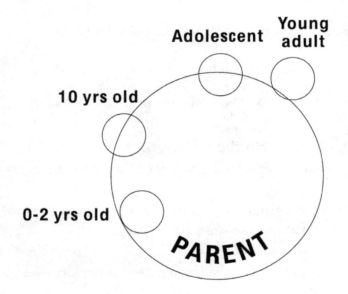

A ten-year-old throws rocks at the neighbor's window from your backyard. Developmentally and with healthy parenting, the child is responsible for this action, which is partially outside of the parent's circle of responsibility. Under the conditions listed, the ten-year-old would know that throwing rocks at a neighbor's window is not an okay thing to do.

If a toddler is up in the attic without close supervision and decides to break the expensive glass Christmas ornaments, that is the parent's responsibility and they must do their best to prevent that situation from happening again.

This diagram is to help parents sort out some of the guilt they carry as a result of their child's inappropriate actions. The diagram is also to help people who were given far too much responsibility when they were younger and feel guilty for their poor judgment, which was probably developmentally appropriate for their age. You may have made a poor parenting call at age thirteen, but ask yourself: why were you put in a position to make a parenting call at this age? Why were there no adults within reach to help you, if you were baby-sitting?

The Mirror

While most of this book has been presenting options about how to protect yourself from outside sources, we are going to address the biggest challenge of all to our inner peace. We have all heard the phrase, "He is his own worst enemy." And we are often able to recognize the enemy within ourselves. In this section, we will be discussing ways to help bring peace within yourself without having to do anything with other people. This is solely about the things you do to trip yourself up and prevent the peace that you want. Throughout the rest of this book, you will be learning to create a mirror that will accurately show you what is going on around you, without you adding the wrong meaning to what you experience around you.

PART 4
THE MIRROR – SEEING THINGS AS THEY ARE

Adding Meaning to Neutral Words

During my workshops, I have presented a series of words that are in the correct order, but are missing punctuation. There are at least two ways to interpret these words in a way that makes sense. The words themselves are neutral stimuli. In other words, without the punctuation, there is no real meaning other than the meaning that you add to it. I will predict that you will add meaning to the words and may even be offended by the statement, but I encourage you to read on so that you can take away a great learning experience. Are you ready?

Woman Without Her Man is Nothing

So many times, I have shown these words that are completely neutral, yet I see so many women folding their arms in front of them. Sometimes I see disapproving looks from some of the men, while there are other men who chuckle. I have even had a woman yell at me in one workshop that she did not have a man in her life and she still knew she was someone.

I assure you that I am not trying to make a sexist slur here. I am only trying to show you how much meaning we can put onto something neutral before we even know the true intent.

Most people when they look at the words without the punctuation automatically assume that the sentence reads in the following way:

WOMAN, WITHOUT HER MAN, IS NOTHING.

Is there another way this can be punctuated?

WOMAN!...WITHOUT HER, MAN IS NOTHING.

If you were able to see this both ways then you are already on your way to understanding where I am going. When you are calm and balanced, then you are able to see things as they are without putting a personal meaning onto the world around us. If you originally thought the words were a sexist slur meant to put down women, then you were attaching a meaning that did not exist. The meaning came from within your circle and, as a result, you created a world in that moment that is against women, which is not real in this circumstance. How many times do we do this? How many times do we make the wrong assumption about the world around us and perceive it as more negative than what we had imagined? How often do we argue to hold onto these negative perceptions?

The advantage to inner peace is that you can see things as they actually are. You are not at the mercy of your reactions. You are not easily manipulated or taken off balance by others. You can accurately assess your situation so you do not have to keep fixing mistakes. There is a sense of calm, focus and happiness as you enjoy the present moment. In martial arts we call this state of mind **one point meditation**.

If you think of this description as being like the flat surface of water, then you can give yourself the image of the quiet mind. The flat surface of the water is a mirror. When you look into a mirror you see the image that is in the world as it really appears to be.

When your mind is not quiet, your mind is like the choppy surface of water. When you look at the images reflected in the water they are distorted. It is difficult to see what you are looking at in the water. When you look at the reflection on the surface of still water then you see things clearly without distortion. You see what is real and can make accurate decisions from this. Your quiet mind serves as an instrument that can measure whether or not something is real. When you are quiet you can detect the people around you who are not quiet and do not have good intentions with greater ease.

The ancient Mayans use to observe the stars in the heavens from towers by constructing large pools of water which would reflect the night sky onto its flat surface.

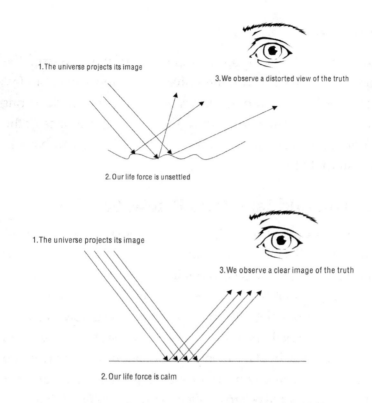

This peaceful state of mind is actually what can make you most effective in a martial arts situation. It is ironic that the peaceful mind is what makes for a successful outcome, but it is true. This is why I study martial arts, because I can find ways to be peaceful in the most chaotic of situations. With a black belt in IAIDO (EE-eye-dough) (Art of the Samurai Sword), I do not ever anticipate I will be walking down the street one day with my sword at my hip and have to defend myself against another person with a sword. If this was my goal, then I would likely be wasting my time. The goal is to become this peaceful mirror state.

Reflection

The Mirror is a test of our alignment with the universe. The more in line we are with the universe, the more we manifest with ease. This awareness allows us to make better decisions with more accurate perceptions. The calmer the surface of the emotional waters within us, the more peace we can have in our external life.

The Emerald Tablet: As Below, So Above

The Emerald Tablet is an historical document that is at least a thousand years old, with translations in Arabic, Latin and English, with the words carved into an emerald stone. There is controversy about how old the Tablet is. The ancient writings on the Emerald Tablet state things are the same below as above. I believe the wisdom of the people who wrote this text had many meanings, but I have one interpretation. They were trying to convey the same concept of the Mirror. Expressed another way, our external lives are a reflection of our internal lives.

Example:

Maybe you know someone who is an artist. They are very creative, high-spirited, full of life and move from one issue to the next. Imagine what their house might look like inside. Although one can never make harsh generalization about everyone all of the time, it is likely that one would be able to guess the look of this person's house. It would likely be colorful, imaginative, with creative projects throughout the home. It may be chaotic with several projects left unfinished or in various stages of the process.

Now imagine the home of an accountant. The house would likely be orderly, organized and have a logical set up that is efficient.

Ways the Mirror Impacts Our World

The first way our Mirror reflects our world is in how we physically manipulate our world. When we have a certain consciousness, then we physically take our circles around our immediate living space and directly manipulate the environment through our physical actions. This happens by hanging pictures, painting the walls and placing the furniture where we have chosen. This happens whenever we do yard work, housework and home improvement. We do this with our space at work as well. We may even have some input with our friends' houses, if they ask us for advice.

The second way we change the world around is us is through our emotions. The next time someone asks how you are doing, respond with "fan-freaking-tastic!" and see how the other person responds. Through sheer emotion you can impact the people around you.

Many times you can see this phenomenon when you visit different organizations. The person in charge is bubbly and energetic, so the people in the rest of the organization are energetic. When the people in charge are angry, then the people below are angry. It seems that whatever is inside of the people running an organization is reflected through the rest of the organization. This is how the Mirror works.

By our own example

The third way we impact our world is through our example. Sometimes our actions cause other people to mimic what we do. There are times when I have dressed up at work and other people start dressing up at work. There are times I bring better quality snacks to work and the quality of snacks from other people begins to improve. There are times with younger people when I have acted in certain ways and they begin to mimic me. None of this happens because I am telling people what to do. Often times there is little or no emotion behind my actions. It is simply a reflection of what is going on with me that seems to create the change in the actions of others. In this same way, other people have the ability to change me through their examples.

I am much less of procrastinator after living with my wife. She is often anxious about deadlines and starts them way before I do. I would always meet my deadlines, but often with a lot of stress. As a result of seeing her example, it is easy for me to meet deadlines in a relaxed way.

The Universe also Reflects Itself Back to You

One time while I was working on the front yard of my house a few years ago, I looked up and down the neighborhood. As I looked up and down the sidewalk, I could see two blocks of sidewalk on my side of the street. I noticed that my section of sidewalk was the only one with debris on it. I suddenly became embarrassed and quickly picked up the debris. Nobody had to tell me to do anything. It was simply the example that everyone was setting that caused me to take action. The more you are aware of this phenomenon and respond to it, the greater peace you have in your life.

Your Intention Impacts the World Around You

Napoleon Hill is one of my heroes. Andrew Carnegie had become the richest man in the world by being a leader in steel production, when Hill had an opportunity to meet him. Early in the twentieth century, Carnegie offered Hill an opportunity to research what makes people successful. Napoleon Hill spent the next twenty years of his life studying people who are now household names: e.g., Henry Ford, Thomas Edison, JP Morgan, along with several presidents just to name a few. What Hill discovered is that these successful men all participated in what he called a "Master Mind" group. He surmised that when two or more people get together to work toward a common goal, then there is a Master Mind that is formed in the "Ethers" that can create what you are looking for in life. Stated another way, when two or more people put their intentions toward a goal, then they create something bigger than the individuals could ever create on their own. In the language of the Circle, this means that what you intend within your circle can be sent out to the universe and reflected back to you, as if you were a mirror. The purer your intent is, the calmer the surface of the water, thus the more potent your power to change the world around you can be. Every group we participate in strengthens the intent that is sent into the universe and our present lives are a manifestation of past intentions.

What groups are you participating in and what are your intentions? Do you get together with other people and complain about the opposite sex? Do you get together with others and work feverishly on a project to make your community a better place? Whatever you choose to do, mixed with your intention behind your actions, creates your manifestations. If you complain then you will get more of the same of what you are complaining about. If you create a project that promotes peace, then you will bring something new to the world that will bring about happiness.

How Do You Create a Mirror within Yourself?

The next few sections offer techniques to that help you maintain inner peace against the most brutal adversary of all: yourself. These methods will help you to remove the obstacles you allow into your circle without the help of other individuals. When the obstacles to your peace are removed, the waters still and you can see clearly what you want to pursue.

Goals

If you want to be happy, set a goal that commands your thoughts, liberates your energy, and inspires your hopes.
—*Andrew Carnegie*

Napoleon Hill spoke passionately about goal setting. He concluded after talking with the most successful people of the last century that properly setting goals is one of the main ingredients for success. What he concluded was something modern day Fortune 500 Company's use called a SMART Goal. SMART is an acronym for the following:

(Specific) - Be clear on what you want and how it is different from everything else in its category.

(Measurable) - It is one thing to say that I want to get in shape, but it is more effective to say that you want to be working out for at least an hour three times a week.

(Attainable) - If you do not believe you can reach your goal then it will take longer to achieve. If you are working on a large deal that is about to happen within the next few days, then it may be appropriate to pursue a million dollars as your goal by the end of the week. If you are making a five-figure salary without any projects happening, then it may not be a good idea to start with such a lofty idea.

(Relevant) - If a goal does not have much meaning in your life then you are not going to be as apt to pursue it. If a goal is close to your heart and relevant to your life, then you are likely to pursue it vigorously.

(Time Specific) - When you say that you intend to reach a goal, your mind has a tendency to say "someday" and the idea can sit there for a long time. When you put a deadline to your goal then your mind adapts and makes the deadline happen. Being Time Specific with your goals is an important step to making sure you are on track with getting what you want from life.

Hill believed that when people set goals it sets up a strong direction, so other forces do not end up interfering with your life. This is the goal of this book — to get people to a point where they are so strong in their intentions they do not need to defend those intentions.

Seeking a Feeling of Spiritual Cleansing

Sometimes the surface of the Mystical Mirror just needs to be cleaned off to reveal its true reflective nature. I have volunteered for various projects throughout my life with various outcomes. I have left some experiences feeling drained and unfulfilled. There was one experience I remember when I volunteered for the Feed My Starving Children organization. I left the house early, in the cold, and was tired when I arrived. I worked on an assembly line to get food to a third world country. I participated in the drudgery to fulfill my obligation and move on with my day. I noticed that something profound happened to me. I began to feel something lift from me. I felt a worn out, negative cloud of energy rise away from me, to be replaced by an energizing breath of fresh air. I felt spiritually clean and positive. This experience helped me to remain calm and to do my job, where I could see more of the good in things without the distraction of traps that usually brought me down. When people showed habits that often bothered me, I was able to let it go and even show a sense of compassion. Other people's bad driving did not seem to take me out of a good mood.

I concluded from this experience that volunteering and performing good deeds is one way we can calm the water's surface and create our Mirror.

Meditation/Prayer

When all else fails, there is always the support of divine intervention. Meditation is the act of quieting your mind to a single thought or no thought. A later chapter discusses some of the techniques to be centered with the universe.

Prayer is a similar technique, depending on your belief system. I am not talking about saying a few words asking the universe for something. I am talking about a soulful connection over a period of time. I am talking about feeling you are making a personal connection with your God or divine source.

If you are an atheist then consider periods of silence. From a scientific aspect, there is evidence that quieting the mind assists in increasing focus, concentration, and decision-making, as well as offering many health benefits. This being in silence also helps you discover who you are away from the status of whatever society holds for you and gets you thinking about what truly makes you different from other people.

Getting quiet and focusing on what is most divine in your belief system is a great way for the surface of the water to calm. Sitting in contemplative prayer or meditation helps to calm the emotional surface of the water. The body at rest helps the mind to be at rest as well as the emotions to be at rest. You do not stir up a bowl of water to get the surface to settle. You let the bowl sit quietly and undisturbed.

This silent mind does not always have to be achieved by just sitting and doing nothing. Throughout much of our history sitting and being present, while completing simple tasks without the noise of multitasking, was a part of everyday life. Shucking corn, sewing, knitting, stirring, painting, sanding, and planting are very common ways people have quieted their minds throughout history. This is why some religions view work as a form of prayer.

Art

Art is a great way to get to the quiet and peaceful state of the Mystical Mirror. When you are working with the medium that is most appropriate for you then it has a calming effect on your spirit. The medium alternatives are endless: painting, sculpting, drawing, writing, and music are some ways to get to that peaceful state.

Moving Meditation

If you are a person who has difficulty sitting still, then there are moving meditation alternatives for you. These are exercises you can do as you are calming your mind. These types of exercises can include walking, yoga, tai chi, labyrinth walks and chi gong. Any type of slow movement can be converted into a moving meditation.

Purging Your Physical Possessions

Within a four-year period, I literally moved my worldly possessions over six times. After the fourth or fifth time of moving the roller blades that I had not used in ten years, I realized that many of my possessions were creating more of a hassle for me than they were worth. I began to purge my belongings and definitely got a greater sense of inner peace. It is amazing the impact this had on me.

Get Right with Yourself

There may have been times we have held onto issues we have with other people or we have to right a wrong we feel we may have done. Whether we are aware of it or not, we carry these wrongs with us and they distort our view of our mirror. We are not able to be as calm because our conscience grinds away at us. We are able to make peace with our wrongs by first admitting we are wrong. Secondly, we need to actually take some action that involves some level of sacrifice on our part to reach our peaceful status. If you are with a gathering and you do not help with picking things up, then you can acknowledge what you failed to do at the gathering and take them out for lunch. If you are late for a meeting then you can buy everyone a snack the next time you meet.

Perhaps the person you have wronged is deceased or the person you wronged has been out of your life for years. You could write a letter of apology to the other person to get your thoughts down. You could wish the other person well in whatever form matches your beliefs, whether it be prayer or positive thoughts. You could help someone out who in some way reminds you of the deceased person you have wronged.

Explore Your Snap Judgments

Many times, we conclude too quickly what we think reality is before we explore it. When you saw the words **WOMAN**

WITHOUT HER MAN IS NOTHING... you may have made a snap judgment that was wrong. It is best to explore when people say things that offend you if that is the meaning that they intended. Sometimes the physical world creates facades that trick us into thinking one thing when another issue exists. An example of this might be if it is sunny outside, then we assume it is warm and we end up being dressed too lightly when we leave home. Exploring the snap judgment would mean that you might step outside before you decide what coat to wear or if a coat is needed.

Forgiveness

The first thing to learn about forgiveness is to have an understanding of what forgiveness is. Forgiveness is not about completely forgetting about what happened when somebody wronged you. Forgiveness is a process where you are able to stop yourself from going down an emotional corridor leading to bad feelings and redirecting yourself back on course. Another way of saying this is you no longer let other people determine your mood.

If you were abused as a child and someone inadvertently reminded you of an aspect of your abuser, then you may have a tendency to relive your experience and take away some bad feelings. If you have truly forgiven your abuser, then the reminder of your abuser would not bring down your emotions.

Forgiving your abuser does not mean you would be best buddies now. It does not mean that you are giving into some idea that what happened to you was right. It merely means you are not going to let the circumstances of the past control your current emotions or actions.

Dignity

I have worked with people of various races, religions, cultures, and ethnic groups. I have the honor of reporting that I have never been labeled as prejudiced or racist. The one underlying aspect that creates peace is treating each other with dignity. When you make sure the basic needs of people are provided and their families are kept safe then the chances of a person having a conflict with you go way down. You can disagree with a person without having to put down their ideas. Most people are looking to save face and be treated with some level of respect.

Many times I had to visit people's homes with the news that their children were misbehaving in school. The reasons were often related to the parents not being able to provide the basic needs for their children. Sometimes this was because the parents were abusing drugs and sometimes it was because they did not know who to trust to ask for help. I offered help with the knowledge that whatever was going on with the parents, they were likely embarrassed I had to come to their home. I had to address the situation compassionately and without judgment.

I could have easily investigated the situation and found plenty of evidence that would prove the parents were bad people. The only problem with this approach is it would not have served to help the children. Proving I was right and taking away the parent's dignity would create non-peaceful feelings toward me, and ultimately everyone would suffer. It is embarrassing to know you cannot take care of your kids. It is embarrassing to know you cannot take care of yourself. Focusing on helping people out of their circumstances restores dignity and restores peace.

When warriors throughout history respected the culture of their enemies, they were able to gain them as allies more quickly. Killing each other on a fair playing field was forgivable while destroying holy relics, violating women and defacing precious art perpetuated conflict. When we maintain the dignity, even of our enemies during a period of conflict, we have a better chance of peace returning more quickly and in a more lasting way.

Strategies to Use Physically to be More at Peace

Physical Exercise

Exercising creates chemicals that positively impact your nervous system. If you are depressed, anxious, and cannot concentrate, then exercise can be a simple and inexpensive solution. Even doing something as simple as walking can be an easy solution to putting you in a better mood. Fresh blood can replenish the corners of your body that can lead to feeling better in subtle ways and enhance your energy. Exercise can enhance your ability to make decisions, focus, and elevate your mood.

Physical Benefits

- Reduce wear and tear on the body.
- Feel better physically
- Your body will be at ease
- Your body will last longer
- Your body will look better

Guard the Senses

An ancient Chinese text "Tao Te Ching" mentions how the ancients emphasized guarding the senses. When you are aware of what is impacting your senses then you can take steps to guard them. You do not always have a choice of what hits your senses, but when you do have a choice you can take steps to protect your senses, thus protecting your inner peace. Your ears register the drone of a dishwasher throughout its cleaning cycle, so you may want to start the dishwasher just before you leave the house. You may want to mute commercials if you are watching TV. You could have some kind of white noise or soft music to drown out sound that impacts your nervous system. The constant flicker of florescent lights can drain your nerves after hours of being subjected to that environment. Your nerves register the million flickers over a long period of time.

Organize

Organizing is similar to guarding the senses, in that you are preventing the impact disorganization has on your nervous system. To look at a straight or curved line has a small and even pleasing impact on the nervous system. To look at a jagged line can have a draining impact on the nervous system over time.

An example of this would be if you had your shoes on the floor and your mail fell off the table. Instead of your eyes just passing over the clean lines of a clear floor, they pause momentarily at the two shoes on the floor and you make a small adjustment while having it in the back of your mind there are shoes on the floor. This is enhanced by seeing the bills on the floor. Somewhere in your mind is the reminder that you have to address each individual bill that is on the floor. If you spend three hours in your home then you probably react to this scenario over a hundred times. This can be an energy drain on the body.

By organizing things, you do not have to think about where you put things. By organizing your bills you can quickly pull out the paper you need from a file, versus spending a few minutes once again searching through the mess on your desk. If you cannot file things like bills or messy projects, then you can at least hide them in containers or storage areas. This means you can look at these items when you want and they do not take away from your inner peace when you do not want them to interfere. Even a squeaky door or a burnt out light bulb can take away energy from your nervous system, so it is important to take the time to fix them.

Many of us stress all year about getting our taxes ready for tax time. It is often there in the back of our minds way before April 15th arrives. One solution to this is to have a folder where you keep all of your tax related items. You buy something that can be deducted on your taxes. When you come home, you put the receipt in the folder. The next time the nervous feeling about taxes comes up, you can tell your mind that it is all in the folder and I can pull it out when I need it. Calm is restored in that moment. When it is actually time to do your taxes you can pull out the folder and know everything is there. This organizational tool can help you to be at peace with one of life's more stressful situations.

Cognitive Strategies for Protecting Your Inner Peace

If you have something you need to bring with you to work or school the following day, it takes some kind of brain space to remember this and that can impact your inner peace. In a this situation, instead of torturing yourself with the thought of forgetting something important, you can just put the item in your car immediately. Other suggestions include putting things in front of the door so you literally have to trip over them as a reminder to take them before you go out the door.

Sometimes when we are dealing with a difficult situation or conflict, we are ruminating about it. We cannot get the thought out of our head, so we spend our time obsessing. Many times we obsess out of fear that we will forget a certain thing if we do not keep it at the forefront of our minds. One solution to protecting your inner peace may be to write these thoughts on paper or in your computer so they do not keep rolling around in your head. We have this understanding of how thoughts can burden us through the language we use.

We say "I have to get this off of my mind" when we have something on our minds. This is the same concept of having burdens in our circle. By liberating the thoughts of your mind, you can reach an inner peace.

Cognitive Benefits

- Clearing your mind of unnecessary thoughts
- Greater concentration
- Necessary focus to work toward your more important goals

Strategies to be Emotionally More at Peace
Emotional Benefits

- Emotional or Physical?

Most scientists agree our bodies produce chemicals that cause us to have physiological urges that serve to maintain the health of our bodies. When our bodies are tired, we have the urge to sleep. Our bodies produce chemicals that make us sleepy and we rest so we can repair the damage of the day. If we ignore this basic urge in the short term, then we get more tired. If we ignore this basic urge in the long term, then we have a higher risk of getting sick. This is true with any of the other basic urges of hunger, thirst, etc. Our bodies intuitively push us to the appropriate response to save ourselves from the basic urge getting worse and when we ignore the urge over time we get sick.

There is another physiological response we have in our bodies and this is emotions. There are all kinds of speculation on what happens to cause us to choose a particular emotion over another. Some people think it is as mundane as the sum total of rewards and punishments. If certain emotions have yielded the avoidance of punishment or yielded rewards, then this is what our brain signals our bodies to produce. On the other end of the spectrum, there are people who think emotions come from a divine source that reaches our hearts. There is a whole debate about this and it is up to each person to decide how they feel about it.

What is clear is that mainstream science believes once an emotion is decided a physiological response then occurs within the body. Chemicals are released to produce the urges to cry, laugh, or get angry. If we choose to ignore the emotional responses, we get sadder, angrier or even want to laugh more. If you let yourself have the emotion, rather than suppressing it, then your body ends up in a healthier state.

For some reason we hold emotions in a different regard. Consider two scenarios. The first scenario is you are alone and you are thirsty.

The second is you are alone and you want to cry.

When we have the physiological response of being thirsty, we think nothing of getting some water. When we have the physiological response of wanting to cry, even when we are by ourselves, we tend to talk to ourselves in negative ways.

"I shouldn't be crying now."

"That is so weak if I cry and I need to be strong."

"If I cry right now, then the person who hurt me wins."

Emotional Bathroom

As important as it is to release your emotions when you have them, it is also important to remember that emotions can be like going to the bathroom. There is a time and place to do it. Although going to the bathroom is a bodily function, we have to excuse ourselves and go to a place that is appropriate. We cannot yell at our bosses, sob in a meeting or fly-off-the-handle when someone wrongs us in traffic without it having some life-changing consequences. We cannot just stop our daily obligations if we are having a bad day. We cannot just up and leave a meeting because we received disappointing news. We have to continue to do the task at hand before we can take an emotional bathroom break. If we get upset due to the actions of others, we cannot just soil the environment with our negative energy. If we do then we suffer the cost of losing relationships and employment.

Predictable Emotions

Emotions come and go. Sometimes the emotion we feel is predictable. We can figure out what the emotion is likely to be due to how it relates to the outside circumstances. Someone throws a cup of water in your face on a cold day and the likely outcome is an angry emotion. Someone close to you gives you a gift you have secretly wanted for a long time and the likely emotion is to be happy. Someone close to you is no longer in your life and your likely emotion is to be sad.

Emotional Storms

Sometimes emotions are not predictable at all. Sometimes emotions come in like storms, without any explanation and without any relation to outside circumstances, and can leave as quickly as they came. Sometimes they linger for days and have nothing to do with outside events. Sometimes there are issues below the surface and sometimes they are just chemical changes. The important thing to remember with emotions is not controlling them, but managing them.

Trying to control the emotional self willfully by manipulative attempts is like trying to choose a number on a thrown die or to push back the water of the Kamo River upstream. Certainly, they end up aggravating their agony and feeling unbearable pain because of their failure in manipulating the emotions.

—Shoma Morita, M.D.

Managing the Storms

The way you manage your emotions is by choosing the best times to take action given your emotional state. If you can avoid important decisions when you are in the middle of an emotional storm, then take the opportunity to address your emotions. Some times when you force yourself to do something during an emotional storm it can leave you doing much more work than doing something after the storm has passed.

It is like trying to rake leaves while the wind is blowing. You might be able to do it, but you are creating a lot of unnecessary work that can be avoided by doing the task at a less stressful time. Sometimes we do not have a choice and have to plug forward during the storm. That is okay too, but you can spare yourself a lot of work when you do have the choice and bring more peace into your life.

Managing your emotions also means that you are good to yourself during the times when the emotional storms hit. This means you accept that this is going to be a rough ride and maybe doing your taxes or starting your new project might not be the best thing to do right now. It is best not to beat yourself up, because you are not being productive. This may even be a perfect time to do something good for yourself. You may have experienced a time when you were trying to get work accomplished under poor conditions and you lose something, or end up painting the wrong side of the wood, or end up deleting an entire file. Sometimes it is best to accept you have to do things slower under poor conditions, if you have to continue to work.

Managing your emotions could also mean, during a particularly bad time, when you are in a biological funk, maybe you can call in a favor to have someone take care of the kids so you can go to your favorite spa or just take a long, quiet walk.

Although it is important to acknowledge your emotions and allow yourself to feel them, it is also important to put them into perspective. When you have a feeling that does not paralyze you, it is important for you to recognize it is there. After that, you can decide to move on and get your work done. You are working on a project and a wave of anxiety over takes you. Think of this wave of anxiety as a cluster of leaves floating on top of a creek. The leaves flow in and, instead of trying to stop the leaves, you let the leaves flow past you until they are all gone. We cannot always control our emotions, but we can let them pass through us. After the emotion has passed we can focus on what we can control, and that is our actions. We can continue to take small steps toward our goals while we make our emotions secondary.

Oxygen Mask Rule

The quotes below all have one theme that is present throughout the ages. We can only be effective if we first take care of ourselves. A simple example of this would be what we are told we need to do if we need an oxygen mask during a flight. If the masks fall and you have a small child with you, who is supposed to get the mask first? The adult is supposed to get the mask first, because if the child passes out while the adult is putting on the mask then the adult can revive the child by putting the mask on the child. If you put the mask on the child first, then you stand a greater chance of both of you dying versus you putting the mask on yourself first. Your chances of you, as the adult, knowing what do in a crisis are much greater than that of your child. You end up being more effective by taking care of yourself first.

This is the first step in protecting your inner peace. You cannot be effective in protecting yourself against others if you cannot protect yourself against yourself. This is often worse than what others do to you. Someone makes an offhanded comment and you ruminate on it all day. You are reliving the moment for hours when it only took seconds to happen. The other person is probably sitting peacefully in their thoughts, without thinking they have done anything wrong. Often times when you confront the person later, you find you misinterpreted the person. The reality is you have been beating up on yourself without anyone really having that intention about you and you have created this negative experience in your day for no reason.

"First remove the plank from your own eye, and then you will see clearly to remove the speck from your brother's eye."
– Matthew 7:5

By first removing the plank from our own eye, the Bible advises us to take care of our own issues first. This relates to the oxygen mask rule of making sure that you have taken care of the issues in your circle first.

O' Sensei

The Art of Peace begins with you. Work on yourself and your appointed task in the Art of Peace. Everyone has a spirit that can be refined, a body that can be trained in some manner, a suitable path to follow.

You are here for no other purpose than to realize your inner divinity and manifest your innate enlightenment. Foster peace in your own life and then apply the Art [of Peace] to all that you encounter.

O' Sensei advises us to look within and foster peace within our own lives before spreading peace to others.

Meditations of Marcus Aurelius

- *A cucumber is bitter. Throw it away. There are briars in the road. Turn aside from them. This is enough. Do not add, "And why were such things made in the world?"* (trans. George Long)

The Roman Emperor Marcus Aurelius suggests that we should handle our affairs without the analysis of why the events keep happening.

"Know Thyself" – Engraved quote at the Temple of Apollo at Delphi

The Greeks believed this to be their most important message, carved at the site that they believed to be the center of the world. The short quote commands us to explore ourselves and to get to know ourselves.

Transforming Anger into Peace

Anger can be one of the most destructive and violent forces on the planet if not channeled properly. I have seen many anger management techniques that talk about counting to ten and taking deep breaths. Others talk about visualizing a peaceful place or trying to see the positive in the situation. I have not found these techniques to be very helpful or effective. This approach can even add to the anger because it does not address what is really going on with a person's emotions.

Anger is rarely an emotion that stands by itself. It is usually a guardian of more vulnerable emotions. Many times, I have heard men proclaim that they are "mad" because their spouse or girlfriend has cheated on them. I make the case they are feeling anger, but it is likely covering up other emotions. The emotions it is covering up are more likely to be about hurt, fear, helplessness, and inadequacy. What often times happens is we experience a situation where we feel we have been weakened in some way. Our response to this is to evoke the powerful emotion of anger. This emotion was very useful in the caveman days when we were attacked or in danger. We would get a burst of energy for the fight or flight response and it would save our lives. This does not work so well, however, if your boss tells you you need to come in on Saturday or the bank teller reports that you have less money in your account than expected.

Infidelity

Going back to the example of infidelity, there is a situation where the person feels weakened as a result of feeling hurt, helplessness, or feelings of inadequacy. The victim of this event must begin to examine their more vulnerable emotions, which are covered up by their anger. Until healing of these other emotions has taken place then anger will likely stay. Talking about these emotions with a trusted friend can help heal the feelings of hurt and helplessness. It is only through looking past the guardian of anger and beyond to the emotions that are beneath the anger that the anger will eventually go away. In doing this you get more control over your emotions and stop reacting to them, thus you have greater inner peace.

You can continue to work on managing your anger by developing the skills to address the areas that are contributing to your feelings of fear, hurt and helplessness. In the example of the unfaithful lover, the victim could create more friendships and connections with other people in the community. By doing this, he is building his skills in connecting with others without having to depend on just one person to provide all of his needs.

A Nurturing Environment

Throughout history, people have lived near the coast, a river, lake, or stream because of the human dependency on water for drinking, cleaning, and food production. They also live close to natural borders and high locations. People do this because it makes their tribe or civilization strong. It is a preventive measure of defense that discourages others from attacking.

It is important to find an environment that nurtures you for the same reason. To find such a place you need to ask yourself a series of questions:

Where do I feel the safest?

Who supports me the most?

Are my basic needs respected at my current location?

Could I continue to grow in my current environment?

What qualities of an environment have served me the best in the past?

What is my gut feeling about all of this?

Exercise
- Go through the previous questions and write down the first answer that comes to mind.
- Identify what you think would be your ideal nurturing environment.
- What could you do to make your current environment more nurturing?
- What goals or affirmations could you post in your environment to help you achieve your dreams?

Medication

If the doctor informed you of a heart condition and you needed to take medication to extend your life, improve your mood, and enhance productivity, would you take it? If you were born with a genetic defect of having an occasional epileptic seizure, would you take medication for it? For some reason most people don't have a problem with answering yes an affirmation in the morning and at night is one of the more result-oriented methods of replacing an unproductive thought with a supportive one. Notice I said replacing instead of a removing. That is because it is very difficult for the mind to not think about something. If I told you not to think of a purple giraffe where does your mind automatically go? So, replacement is important. Make the new statement as believable as possible.

Example
You might replace a thought of poverty with a thought of prosperity. Replace: Nice guys always finish last in business. Repeat: The more helpful I am to my customers, the more money I'll make. You are still being nice in this example, but in the second example the "niceness" works in your favor.

Exercise
- Think of your dearest wish and write it down, without any regard as to the reality of its manifestation.
- Think of the steps you need to take to make it feasible.
- Observe the thoughts that come forth to stop you from reaching your dreams.
- Write down the thoughts that stop you from pursuing the goal.
- Write a victorious response to your negative thoughts.
- When a limiting thought happens, state the victorious response three times. Practice this for one week as the thoughts occur.

Exercise
- Think about a current temptation you are experiencing.
- Visualize how you would feel after following through. Think of all the outcomes — minutes, hours, days, and months after.
- Think about how your decision would impact the people closest to you.
- Think about how following your temptation would impact your children.
- Decide whether your life would be better or worse for the experience.

Confronting Temptation

This technique is similar to the "so what" approach. A friend, who happened to be a therapist, asked me about my weekend. I started talking about how I didn't get to finish all of my yard work. I had planned to maybe prune some more of the bushes in the back. He asked me if I would feel tremendously better if I had accomplished all of these tasks. After an honest and courageous inventory of my thoughts, I had to admit that I really would not have felt all that much better, even if I had met every one of my expectations.

This method can also be similar to the ones used in handling your emotions.

Let your mind become flooded with the tempting thought. Instead of using all of that energy to hold it back, by telling yourself that it is not a big deal, just let it loose. Notice the peaceful thoughts that rush into your mind and the exhilarated feeling that comes from it. Allow whatever emotion you feel to be conscious. It is already part of you, so why not be conscious of it? This may be the only available way for you to expel such a powerful thought. Follow through with the thought to its logical conclusion. If you have this burning desire to smack someone, first think about how satisfying it would feel for that person to get what they deserve and the surge of conquest in your veins. Then think about the gasps you would hear throughout the room, accompanied by looks of judgment regarding your inappropriateness. Think about how you would feel as the police handcuff you in front of children and people you respect. Think about how people would acknowledge you with polite discomfort even years after the event.

The Enemy Within

Before you can defend yourself against attacks from another person you must learn to protect yourself from the most formidable enemy of all. The opinion that matters most to any of us is the opinion we hold about ourselves. If a record-breaking athlete was told how terrible he was by a random stranger on the street, then the athlete would most likely laugh at the stranger. He would not feel the need to defend himself, because his opinion of himself is strong enough. He would not waste his energy with such endeavors. He knows he is the best, feels it in his heart, and moves on toward more important things. This would be true of most people in their strongest areas; if they have a strong enough belief in themselves they do not need to be validated with external awards or measurements of praise.

This higher position of being so spiritually strong you do not feel the need to defend yourself is the goal of this book.

The Generous Benefactor Question Part I & Part II

What thoughts are the most destructive? Probably the ones you do not know, those in your subconscious mind. When you are not aware of these destructive thoughts they secretly linger and weave their obstacles into your life. This exercise that will help bring those demons out in the open. These are the thoughts that keep you from following your heart's desire and get in the way of your inner peace.

Part I

Think about what you want to do more than anything else, as if you did not have any limitations to do so — in other words, if there was no limit to financial resources, or access to people who can make things happen for you. It may be writing children's books, making music, making movies, educating the world on important topics or helping people throughout the world. Whatever it is you want to do would be happening on a grand scale. This is something that touches your heart deeply, that lights you up with passion. It would be helpful to write this down, because we often have a perception of what we want without being able to articulate it. Even trying to say it aloud can be difficult and will help us define our goals.

You find yourself in a situation where a representative of a major investor/power broker approaches you; they want you to follow through on your dream job. This would be someone along the lines of Oprah Winfrey or Bill Gates. You now have everything available to you to fulfill your dreams. This investor would finance every aspect of your dream job and they would provide you with the resources and connections to make it happen. You would be supplied with the best advisers, marketing talent, and people at the top of your profession to do whatever it is to make it work for you.

What are the thoughts and emotions that are coming up for you at this time? Write them down and see what happens. What thoughts came up for you?

These are usually the thoughts that keep us from pursuing our dreams. There is usually an emotion of fear and self-criticism. We tell ourselves we do not know enough, we are not educated enough, and we could not possibly pull this off.

These are the unhealthy monsters of our past, interfering with our peace. These issues often stay with us the rest of our lives and need to be examined and kept in their place. Unfortunately, most people try to put their issues behind them without examining them. The sad result of this is people become paralyzed in their lives without ever moving forward.

They end up living the same day over and over again. The monsters end up ruling them, because many people try to pretend there is nothing wrong in their life.

Ways to Face Your Demons

The other way of addressing the enemy within is to explore the source of your sad feelings and irrational negative thoughts. Maybe there was a message you heard from your parents or teachers in your early childhood. Maybe a trauma or the bad outcome of a decision placed negative thoughts about yourself in your mind that have not gone away.

The Twelve Step Programs encompass a spirit of looking at ourselves honestly and turning our problems over to a higher power. The issues that come up for people during the steps are what need to be addressed. Someone we are close to can be a great resource for this activity. Listen to the messages people are telling you. Is there some truth to what they are saying? A lot of times there might not be any truth to what they are saying, but people will make misperceptions as a result of the image you present. The image you present may not be consistent with the reality of who you are.

A good friend is someone you can ask to get honest answers and reflect back to you the reality of who you are. Sometimes your needs may require more than what a friend can give; something more is needed. A therapist can be a good alternative to let a non-judging stranger be a sounding board who can articulate healing steps toward peace that have shown to be successful with other people.

Part II

There is another part of this opportunity that brings forth some very helpful issues that could very well lead you to the success you want. These questions would address the weaknesses in the areas where you need to make improvement. Maybe you need to hone your skills in certain areas. Maybe you know what works in your profession, but lost track of where the actual research is that supports your cause. Maybe you need the numbers as a demonstrated proof to strengthen your position with the doubting people you are likely to face.

I realized when I wanted to spread the philosophy of this book that many areas needed to be strengthened and polished to reach the level of quality I desired. I started strengthening my commitment to martial arts and started looking at the different opportunities in public speaking. I researched publishers and went to book expos. It takes some courage to admit that you are not doing everything to the best it can be done and take the actions to fix what needs to be addressed.

It also takes more than just facing your weaknesses. It means you also have to take action steps to address them. You need to get stronger if you want to enjoy the peace you desire in your life.

Strengthen Your Position

He who knows how to live can walk abroad

Without fear of rhinoceros or tiger.

He will not be wounded in battle.

For in him rhinoceroses can find no place to thrust their horn, Tigers, no place to use their claws,

And weapons, no place to pierce. Why is this so? Because he has no place for death to enter.
–Lao Tsu

The following techniques are general ways to enhance your ability to defend yourself. They are a good foundation for the actual block and to strengthen your ability to shield yourself from impact. In martial arts it is important to first learn stances, because without the proper stance then your blocks and strikes become powerless.

In Martial Arts
"A good stance and posture reflect a proper state of mind."
–O'Sensei

A good stance in martial arts is very much like living your life with integrity. A good stance is a solid starting place where things begin to happen. Let me demonstrate this in a non-martial arts forum.

The answers to life's most complex problems are relatively easy if you do not consider the strong position you need behind it.

Example:
If you have an addiction to something, then just stop the addictive behavior.

If you want to lose weight just eat less and exercise more.

If you want to make more money, then work more hours and try different business ideas.

If you have feelings of loss or trauma, just put it out of your mind.

It easy to see from these examples that these solutions require a strength of character or a particular stance as a starting point in order for these overly simplistic approaches to work. The challenge in reaching our goals is blocking out the things that interfere with them.

Living Life with Integrity

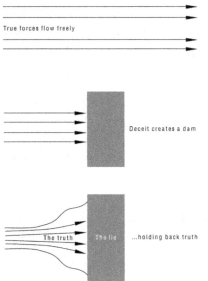

Getting in touch with who you are and what you are is one thing; living your life according to your true self is another. Truth, as you find it, is a powerful force of change.

The Truth ...Holding Back Truth

Truth is a force in the universe that can transform the world. When people in therapy are confronted with the truth they either transform their lives into something more fulfilling or they run away, desperately guarding their denial.

When people deceive themselves or others truth does some very interesting things. Imagine a river flowing steadily. The river represents truth in all of its forms; i.e., true emotions, true words, true actions etc. Now imagine something untrue blocking this river like a dam. The truth will be shielded temporarily, but truth will always find a way to seep out. Either you will begin to see leaks in the dam or, eventually, you will see truth spilling over the dam. When the deceit is able to hold back the truth for a long time, truth builds like a tremendous lake behind the lie. No matter how well orchestrated the lie is, the dam will eventually give way to this powerful force of truth built behind it. The lie will come crashing down quickly, dramatically, and often without warning. This is the stuff of historical revolution — the stuff of life-changing revelation. The dam must come down.

The analogy relates to emotions as well. You can only hold back your feelings for so long before they leak out or spill over the dam with which you block them.

It might sound a little obvious, but when you are living your life consistent with your purpose you have less to think about. You don't have to remember the lie you told and how your next move might blow your cover. Living life with integrity is one of the most positive ways of keeping your circle clear of many unwanted thoughts. It is the ultimate armor for your circle. Integrity is the purest form of character a person can reach. The more purifying the energy, the faster your circle will be cleared of any debris that any force attempts to place within the borders of your circle. In most cases, opposing forces cannot penetrate the perimeter with a strong shield of integrity defending it.

Integrity

Integrity has the benefit of appearing strong because you are strong. There is no juicy weakness or scandal to expose. There is not a skeleton to find. When people attack individuals who possess character, the attackers are often the ones who end up with anxiety.

Integrity is comparable to holding a proper stance in martial arts. When you squat with your knees bent a person trying to kick your knee could break their own foot. Standing sideways with your hands in front of the vulnerable areas of your body increases your safety. When someone takes a strong hold on his or her morality, we call it taking a "stance" on an issue. In martial arts, standing properly and exhibiting integrity share the same advantages. Ultimately, you are less vulnerable to attacks when you follow this practice because you are in the best position to defend yourself. If someone falsely attacks your character you will have evidence, friends, and witnesses available for your defense. In a proper stance you will have the strongest parts of your body in the best places to most easily block incoming attacks.

Imagine how much more powerful the politicians and celebrities in our lifetime would be had they had better character. If you look at all of the great societies, governments, companies, and organizations you will see a collection of character words that serve as the foundation. Walk through all of the historical monuments of Washington, DC and observe how many times you see words such as:

JUSTICE, STRENGTH, HONOR AND TRUTH.

Look for these words as you notice other cultures or organizations you encounter.

Take Charge of Your Life so Others Won't!

Along with integrity is taking charge of your life. When you think about how much control others have over your life, there isn't much others can force you to do. As long as you follow some basic codes of conduct and the golden rule, you have a lot of freedom to do what you want. Imagine, within your circle, you have some authority figure exerting some control over your space. This authority could be a boss, parent, teacher, customer, or law enforcement officer. When a person does not control their behavior and violates the rights of others that person often seeks or is forced to accept other forces in their life to control them. A probation officer requires regular check-ins or technological devices are attached to a person that track your whereabouts. Most of your day is still under your control, but you have to keep your probation issues in mind. If you try to rebel against your probation officer, authorities will order in the assistance of the law or mental health professionals. Authority takes charge of your space because you did not control yourself. If you try to beat authority and try to scare them off with intimidation, your probation officer takes you to the judge, who sentences you to jail and full psychiatric treatment. Now, prison guards tell you what to do for most of your day and control most of what happens within your arms' reach. Others control most of your circle because you were unable to control your actions.

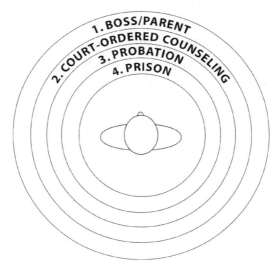

There are even more subtle versions of this. When you do not take charge of your life then other people follow up on your actions. If you have to be reminded to do things all of the time or if you put what is your obligation onto other people's circles, then there are more subtle consequences that interfere with your peace. There is a constant sense of checking up on the other person and second-guessing. All of your talents and credibility are diminished.

Keeping in Line

When we are consistent and organized we untangle our thoughts and move them into a straight line. Imagine if you organized a set of twelve pipes in a straight line, starting with the biggest pipe closest to you. The second biggest pipe would follow behind the biggest. You clearly labeled the size of each pipe and fitted them together from 12" down to 1". Someone asks you for the 8" pipe and you can find it instantly. You could quickly recognize if any of the pipes were stolen or damaged. If you were a surgeon, wouldn't you want all of your instruments organized with the largest instrument on one end and the smallest on the other? Wouldn't you want the instruments you use the most to be closest to you?

Let's look at the opposite set up. You have twelve unmarked pipes thrown together in a small box. You receive a request for an 8" pipe and you have to fish around for it while figuring out the size. You would not be able to recognize if a pipe was missing or damaged as easily as when the pipes are set in a straight line. The organization and alignment increases your efficiency.

Organize your thoughts in a similar way by keeping the most important issues closest to you and line up issues of lesser importance away from you.

The Wheel of Good Fortune

What you may discover is you may need to create several lines that move away from you, like spokes of a wheel. One line might be labeled family; another might be labeled career. Health, recreation, social world, and personal projects are all parts of you creating the very spokes to the wheel of your circle. The physical properties of adding spokes to the wheel make the circumference significantly stronger. Another physical characteristic of spokes is if one is significantly stronger than the other then the wheel is more likely to sustain damage at the location of the weaker spoke.

These physical principals are also true for the circle that surrounds your space. If one area of your life is weak it can weaken your entire position.

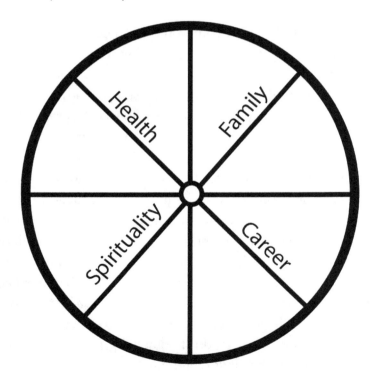

Example: If you are financially successful, but have poor health (maybe even just a toothache), the quality of your life will suffer tremendously. Conversely, if you have perfect heath, but have a burdensome financial difficulty (an unpaid utility bill or foreclosure), your life will be filled with anxiety that will negatively impact all areas of your life.

Keep all areas of your circle in balance. Keep all lines straight and organized like the spokes of a wheel and you will stay strong. Because you can quickly align issues that go astray and recall information quickly, you have the advantage over forces that work against you.

In a financial situation, you would balance your accounts regularly and log your transactions. When you organize your finances you can recognize problems in the early stages and fix them easily. When someone accuses you of not paying your bills you can quickly provide evidence to prove them wrong in the form of a properly filed canceled check.

Organization and alignment are easy qualities to spot in the business world, but what about in a family situation? Align with your family by maintaining regular contact with family members. Know the parents and phone numbers of all of the friends of your kids. Know what your spouse's dreams are and carefully observe the interactions of all family members. You will react more quickly when something is affecting your loved ones. It will be easier (remember I said easier, not easy!) for you to know what to do if something goes wrong, because you know the details of the situation. Congruency is the approach for success in this situation. Irresponsible gambling would be incongruent with a harmonious family life, whereas honoring your agreements would be a congruent act.

When someone is congruent we use expressions such as, "She's in line with this department" or "He's being straight with me." When someone is incongruent we say that the person is "crooked" or getting off track.

By following these steps and organizing the spokes of your wheel, your circle will become stronger. You will be able to freely pursue your desires and make it more difficult for outside forces to attack. When molecules are in line in a piece of iron the metal attracts other metals. When your actions are aligned with your dreams you attract the physical manifestations of those dreams.

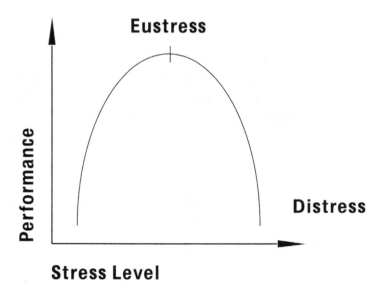

Balance

A martial artist incorporates both the yin and the yang; two forces that complement each other. Yin is the feminine energy and yang is the masculine energy. We see numerous examples of this model in nature: night/day, heaven/ earth, giving/ receiving, creation/destruction. A martial artist does not think in terms of good vs. evil. A martial artist does his/her best to create balance and harmony between the two forces by following the central line of the symbol. You do not want to go too extreme into one force or the other, unless that action is needed to balance out an already unbalanced circumstance.

Martial arts require your moves start from a balanced stance and as one limb goes up, the other comes down to protect any openings. If both of your arms went up you would expose your ribs and heart to potentially negative forces.

In our everyday lives we require balance, particularly when it comes to stress. This point is made abundantly clear in Hans Seyle's concept of eustress. This is the level of stress that provides you with optimal performance. When you do not have enough stress in your life your pace tends to take on a lethargic quality. As stress increases, your efficiency is optimized — up to a point.

When you exceed that optimal performance point you move into what is called "distress." This is the fumbling "forget where you put things" kind of panic that creates problems in any undertaking.

What we can take from this is we need to relax. Most people, when they fail to accomplish a task, tend to move toward distress. They are not in harmony and need balance in their lives. Often, when others fail, people will scold, punish, or criticize. This only adds stress to the situation and tends to be counterproductive. By helping the other individual to relax you are more likely to get the desired results. Sadly, many of us are conditioned to punish what we term "bad" behavior.

Turn on Your Radar

Radar is your vigilant awareness of the world outside of your circle. It is checking out where the exits are in a building or keeping you informed of situations that could have an impact on your life. It informs and updates information about everything in your environment. When something comes at your circle out of left field, you can make a more informed decision and address it.

Stay Under the Radar

Many of our honest mistakes can go unnoticed if we stay under the radar. Show up to work on time, do what you are supposed to do, and keep the complaints to a minimum. Maintain an organized work area and live your life with integrity. If you arrive late, make waves, and earn a bad reputation, the magnifying glasses come out and many will analyze your every move.

Play

Play is doing something that is enjoyable to you that is fun to do. This means you are not allowed to produce anything or accomplish something unless it involves reaching a goal in a sport. We are holistic beings and when we do not play, part of ourselves punishes the other part. I do not like to use the word inner child, but I don't have a better one. If this part of you doesn't get its needs met, other areas will be sabotaged. If you won't let me have a good time, then I won't let you work!

Examples of Playing

Everyone has a different version of what play is. Play is basically doing something without the need to produce something. It is with the intent of having a good time. It is different than just passing the time. Many times, we substitute play for filling our time. This means surfing the internet, playing another game of solitaire, or watching a million reruns. It is safe and does not require a lot of effort. It does not leave you fulfilled.

Play is more deliberate. It is actively choosing to set aside some time with the intent of having a good time. For some people play may look like tossing a Frisbee with friends, while others might get excited about reading the latest novel that just came out. Stamp collecting, sports, hiking, dancing, puzzles, and various forms of art are just some ways people can play.

Stopping Guilt

Sometimes guilt can weaken our position and we need to address it before it bogs us down too much. When guilty feelings are present, it is important to stare the situation right in its face.

Decide which actions you could have controlled and which actions were unpredictable outcomes of an unfortunate situation. Were your actions reasonable, given your understanding of the situation?

After this search, you may discover you are at fault. Offer amends to those impacted by your bad decisions. You cannot control the reactions of others, but you can remove the suffocating issue from your circle. Sometimes owning your indiscretion can be a very healing act for the victim of your actions, even if it happened a long time ago. It is always good to follow up apologies with actions of reconciliation. There may be no way to repair your damage, but an action demonstrates you are willing to sacrifice, which offers more peace to the situation.

Sometimes we feel guilty about larger social issues; e.g., poverty, illiteracy, hunger, environmental issues, etc. Take action to satisfy your guilt. Donate money if you can afford to do so or volunteer your services to a worthy charity.

Guilt may also be a sneaky form of resentment. You may feel guilty about not performing at your job, because you resent your decision to take the job. You may resent your decision to enter a bad relationship out of pity; but, on the surface, you feel guilty for your thoughts of wanting to get out of it. Explore these channels of guilt.

Does It Really Matter?

Many have found this technique to be most helpful when thoughts of guilt have invaded their personal game spaces. When guilty thoughts begin to nag you about all of the things you should have done during the week ask yourself the question, "So what?" When you start thinking you spent too much time watching TV or talking to friends, again, ask yourself "So what?" Is it really going to compromise your current lifestyle if the vacuuming is done tomorrow instead of today? Give yourself a break.

Most things that are left undone aren't really going to ruin someone's life because they were done one day after you anticipated something. So you spent much of the weekend sleeping...So what? Maybe you had a long, difficult week. Maybe your brain knows when it needs to take a break and shuts down, without telling your conscious mind. It's okay. So what if you forgot something at the grocery store. Everybody makes mistakes and you will make mistakes in the future. If the people around you cannot understand, they need to own the problem, not you. Ask yourself the next time you get angry with yourself for not doing what you had wanted to accomplish how much it really impacts your circle.

Become the Observer

When someone asks us who we are, what do we think to tell the other person? We often discuss title, or status, our label and what we have accomplished. This is not who we are. What makes us different from other people who have the same accomplishments? Is it the way we react to things? Do we have to react? One of the great ways to tap into this great power of insight is to practice the observing consciousness. The best way to explain this is through a story.

When I worked as a counselor in a group home I took a group of residents to the circus. One of the clients was blind and requested I narrate the events, as they were happening. The dialogue went something like this:

"There is a young lady climbing a rope and reaching for a trapeze. She is swinging on the trapeze and has just flipped in the air. Her partner caught her...there is a group of elephants and they are swinging their trunks as they parade out into the arena..."

This kind of narration went on for a couple of hours. When I was getting ready for bed after this continued dialogue, I would hear the narration in my head.

"I'm walking upstairs to the bathroom. I grab my toothbrush and start brushing my teeth. I look for a washcloth. I grab the washcloth and soap and wash my face."

I hadn't realized it at the time, but I was practicing the observing consciousness. I was stepping back from myself and objectively narrating my actions. I found this technique to be quite helpful in crisis situations, as a therapist.

Not only was I observing my actions, but I could also step back and look at my emotions. I could observe how my emotions influenced the situation I was in and how my body changed with each emotion. When I can observe my thoughts, feelings and actions, I can have a clearer idea of what is happening in the world around me. The observing consciousness is the stabilizing force that flattens out the ripples of our liquid essence and allows us to see the world's truths — much like a placid lake reflects an accurate picture of the world above it.

Here's a practical application of this. When you are in a situation where someone pushes your buttons and you don't want them to control you, here is what you do.

"I am listening to this person explain the computer to me. They are talking to me like I'm a three year old. He just rolled his eyes at me and my heart is beginning to beat faster. I am starting to breathe heavier and my face is getting warm. I take a deep breath. I realize I am very smart and even though he is talking to me condescendingly, I am listening to the part I need to understand."

The advantage to this practice is you can turn your reactions into choices. You can have greater control over what lies within your circle and thus a greater advantage in a given situation. Your own self-awareness gives you a place to start and your calmness allows you to make choices.

I was able to step out of myself and realize there was more to me than just my body. Whether you call it a soul, mind, or just my thoughts, there is something more to me than just my body that remains the same regardless of my physical circumstances. I may feel pain or pleasure, but they are only parts of my body. The observer remains untouched by the experiences of the body.

Abandon Expectations

This is the most personally challenging technique for me to follow. In other words, set goals, but do not base your emotions on the outcome of the events. So many times I have interviewed for jobs I thought would be great, only to find out I did not get it. My mood then goes into a tailspin, because my mood becomes reliant on the outcome of the interview. Being the observer helps with this struggle. I am happiest when I am not betting my mood on what the universe decides for me. I have always been taken care of when I listened to my intuition more often than when I forced a direction with the outcome determining my mood. Be wary of the signs that show we are putting our faith in external things. Be mindful of the behaviors of checking your email constantly and having the urge to pester others in order to get what you want. Once you recognize these events happening, try moving in a completely different direction.

Be More Open

"Empty your mind, be formless, shapeless like water. You put water into a cup, it becomes the cup. You put water into a bottle, it becomes the bottle. You put it into a teapot it becomes the teapot. Now water can flow or it can crash. Be the water my friend."

–Bruce Lee

There are lots of times when we have allowed too much to happen to ourselves by letting our guard down, sometimes with devastating results. There is also a consequence for shutting too many things out of your life. If you are too skeptical then you can keep a lot of opportunities from coming your way. Being too rigid keeps the flow of life from happening to you. So many times in my career I have heard people holding onto their inaccurate beliefs and it does not matter how much they are suffering as a result of their beliefs, they refuse to let go of those beliefs.

I have seen people create more chaos and struggle in their life due to making sure everything lines up perfectly. It is adapting to the constantly changing nature of the world that leads to inner peace. I always have an audiobook in my car in the event that I am stuck in traffic. If someone changes what they had requested of me, then I change. For inner peace, I remember Bruce Lee saying, "...Be the water my friend."

State Change

In our goal-focused culture we have all of these sayings about staying on task and not giving up on our goals. Sometimes we do need to take breaks. Sometimes resolving a computer issue we have been working on for hours is not as emotionally satisfying as going swimming or bicycling. This is because our bodies need to change our physical state of being in order to change our mental state of being. After I have written all day I like to roll on the mats of an Aikido class to shake my body out of that boring sedentary state of writing into the lively activities of being thrown through the air.

Create Something

When I was younger I was always bored and looking for ways to be entertained. As I got older I realized I would never have to be bored, because there is always something I can create. Making new creations with the intention to make the world a better place is a way to go to your peaceful state. Destruction is a force of agitation and creation is a force of peace. The next time you create something notice how you feel when you are finished.

When I work on creative projects that are directly in line with my inner goals, I experience a similar phenomenon to that which I had when I volunteered. When I start a creative project that nagging sensation starts to go away. I start to feel a sense of ease, as the thought of what I want to create actually appears before me in physical form. I do not have to keep running the thoughts through my head when my creation is sitting there before me.

Three Questions

There is a whole Eastern therapy that focuses on three questions that help others be more mindful of the positive things that happen in a person's life. These questions can help you to find peace in a past or currently troubling relationship. I encourage you to follow through on answering these questions and, if it works for you, then I would encourage you to explore the deeper meanings behind Naikan Therapy. The three questions are:

- What have I received from _____ ?
- What have I given to _____ ?
- What troubles and difficulties have I caused _____ ?

Talk to Someone

Sometimes the act of discussing the issues that are bothering you can do wonders for calming the choppy waters of your Mystical Mirror. Sharing the more vulnerable parts of yourself, with the intention of healing, is a powerful act. Many times the solutions to your problems become apparent as you articulate the words that come out of your mouth. The clear answer was waiting for you to get the fuzzy mess of negative thoughts swirling around in your head and put them into words. When you share with trusted people, then you have the opportunity to share resources.

Many times that deep sharing with a trusted friend provides the healing you need. Sometimes knowing you are not alone in your trials and that someone understands what you are experiencing is part of the healing as well. Other times it is just good to have a friend who says they will support you no matter what, even if they have no understanding of what you are going through.

Sometimes your friends are not equipped to discuss the problems you have and they just do not know what to do, despite their loving acts of kindness and support. It is during these times someone else is needed to help you. Talking to a trained professional can create a whole new life for us. I have seen people transformed from rigid, angry symbols of tortured souls into bright healing spirits that help others. There is no need to walk around in emotional pain. With an ounce of healing you can have gallons of fulfillment in your life. This is not a situation where you have to have a serious psychological disorder in order to get the help. It can just be a circumstance where you are in pain.

Life Coaching

Often times we experience being in stuck in our lives and it has nothing to do with a major issue from our past. Sometimes we want to move past a place of being mediocre into a place of greatness. Life coaching can provide you the tools to develop your own inner guidance to make the right choices toward that greatness.

Life coaching helps you stay accountable, stay focused on your goals and break down your goals into the weekly you steps you need to achieve them. If you want to move out of rut and into that "alive" space of peace, then you may want to consider life coaching.

Gratitude

Thank you for following me in this journey of peace. Part of getting to that place of peace is through appreciation. This way of thinking sets up a feeling that brings about more of what we appreciate. If we appreciate what a person does they are more likely to more of the same. I believe our world responds in the same way and makes the surface flat.

The Mirror is Your Best Friend

Keeping the emotional waters calm within your circle in the midst of a potential conflict is the best defense that you have. When you stay calm your opponent sees a clear image of themselves in the flat surface of your emotional waters. This sometimes leads to an escalation of emotion in the other person at first, but subsides quickly in most cases. Often times people will figure out during the conflict that you are not fighting with them and they spontaneously admit their own faults. If you were yelling back at the person then they may only hear your yelling and not hear their own yelling. Your calm mirror state helps them to see themselves. There is also no fuel for the fire of conflict. If you are not fighting back then there is no energy the other person is getting from you.

It has been my experience that people are more apt to go along with what you want when you remain calm during the conflict. When your opponent is the only one yelling your opponent is more likely to see what they have done wrong and make apologies sooner. When you yell back once, after the person has yelled at you twenty times, it is enough to keep peace from happening.

Reflecting your opponent's image back to him is more than just sitting there. Reflecting is calmly telling the person your direct observations.

Here is a real life example:

I had a teenager tell me to "stick it" (and I am censoring) when doing a group activity. I remained calm and continued with the group activity. A few minutes later the same teenager told me the "snobs" at her school did not like her, because she was poor. I reflected back to her that I was not able to tell if she was poor, but I did notice she told me to "stick it" earlier during the session. I also pointed out that might be a more likely reason why people might not like her than her being poor. At a later time the teenager approached me and confided in me about many things in her life that were happening. She apologized through her tears and thanked me for pointing out the truth about her behaviors. By using this technique of being a mirror I did not have to defend myself. She was able to see her own issues clearly in the flat peaceful surface I had created.

Summary
Someone at my church gave me a poem of theirs that summarized the essence of my book in one paragraph.

It is my goal to live in peace and let others do the same.

I will honor myself by being responsible for me and my actions. I will honor you by recognizing that you are responsible for yourself and your actions.

We can only be responsible for our actions, not the results. May God bless both of us.

Elliott Wurtzel © 2001

The Ultimate Goal

Now you have learned some techniques about how you can protect your inner peace. You can start thinking about the ultimate goal of having peace in your life all of the time. Will you achieve it all of the time? Probably not. But you will be able to recognize when you get off track sooner. You will be able to get yourself back on track a lot faster and again head toward inner peace. Your "boat" will not be as easily rocked, meaning it will require more negative events to disturb your peace. You will begin to see the positive parts of things, without denying the darker side of things.

When I did home visits for my job as a social worker I saw and experienced many negative things. I saw drug paraphernalia, empty liquor bottles, gang members, people getting arrested, gunshots fired, doors slammed in my face, bullet shells in the street, syringes on the lawn. With all of that in mind I was able to see a lot of good, even under the worst of these circumstances. I had many people hurry me into their homes to get me out of the rain or cold. I saw Bibles open up in the living rooms of many homes I visited. Someone gave me a coupon to a store for giving her a ride to her daughter's school. Many people thanked me for the work I did. I might get the occasional person on the street asking me for a dollar, but most people said hello to me with a smile. The school resource officers I worked with were fearful of going into these neighborhoods where many law enforcement officers/deputies lost their lives.

I was able to walk without fear and had relatively peaceful interactions, even under these circumstances. I believe that this happened because I went beyond the techniques of having to "defend" or "protect" my inner peace. I just try to live in peace while being the mirror. When I am able to get in this space then I am able to have fewer conflicts and more positive experiences, with people actually trying to help me out. It is my wish that everyone can reach the place where peace becomes such a large part of their lives that there is nothing that can stop it.

I believe that inner peace happens when we connect with whatever we think is our source in life. Many people think the source of their life is God or the Universe, while others feel the source of their life is their personal freedom and claiming their greatness. I hope that you have some more tools to help you stay connected with your source. I hope that the source within is so big that you do not feel that you have to protect it any more.

Imagine a world where people kept their word and took care of the responsibilities that belonged to them. Imagine what that would be like, if you fostered a sense of inner peace, and how that would impact the world around you as well as the other people in your life. You can be a better person to your family, your co-workers, your community, your country, and your world.

All life is a manifestation of the spirit, the manifestation of love. And the Art of Peace is the purest form of that principle.

A warrior is charged with bringing a halt to all contention and strife. Universal love functions in many forms; each manifestation should be allowed free expression. The Art of Peace is True democracy.

– O' Sensei - Founder of Aikido

Resources/References

998 "Report Card on the Ethics of American Youth; Survey Data on Youth Violence." (1999, May) [Bellsouth.net]. Josephson Institute of Ethics.

http://www.josephsoninstitute.org/98-survey/violence/98survey-violence/htm [2000, May 7].

Adler, R. B. & Towne, N. (1984). *Looking Out Looking In* 4th Edition (pp. 352-359). New York, NY: CBS College Publishing.

Alexander, Matthew (2008). *How to Break a Terrorist: The U.S. Interrogators Who Used Brains, Not Brutality, to Take Down the Deadliest Man in Iraq.* New York, NY Free Press.

Christakis, N. & Fowler, J (2009). *Connected: The Surprising Power of Our Social Networks and How They Shape Our Lives.* New York, NY: Little, Brown & Company.

Elkind, D. (1998). *Character Education: An Ineffective Luxury? Child Care Information Exchange.* 124, p.6.

Fisher, R. & Ury, W. (1991*).* *Getting to Yes: Negotiating Agreement Without Giving In* 2nd Edition: Negotiating Agreement Without Giving In. New York, NY: Penguin Books.

Gibbs, L. E. (1991). *Scientific Reasoning for Social Workers: Bridging the Gap Between Research and Practice* (pp. 10-13). New York, NY: MacMillan Publishing Company.

Glasser, MD, Glasser, William (1998). *Choice Theory: A New Psychology of Personal Freedom.* New York, NY: HarperCollins Publishers, Inc.

Hart, G., (2005) *The Routledge Dictionary of Egyptian Gods and Goddesses* (p. 158). Routledge, second edition, Oxon.

Hill, Napoleon (1937). *Think and Grow Rich.* New York, NY: Fall River Press.

Kowalewski, Paul J., *Human Communication: A Transactional Perspective: SUC at Fredonia*, NY, 1983.

Krech, Greg (2002). *Naikan: Gratitude, Grace and the Japanese Art of Self-Reflection.* Berkley, CA: Stone Bridge Press.

Lee, Bruce&Linda (1975). *Tao of Jeet Kune Do.* Santa Clarita, CA: Ohara Publications, Inc.

MacLaren, Catharine (2005). *Rational Emotive Behavior Therapy: A Therapist's Guide* (2nd Edition), Impact Publishers.

Melchizedek, Drunvalo (1998). *The Ancient Secret of the Flower of Life Volume 1*. Flagstaff, AZ: Light Technology Publishing.

Morita, Dr. Shoma (Translated by Peg Le Vine) (1998). *Morita Therapy and the True Nature of Anxiety-Based Disorders*. Albany, NY: State University of New York Press.

Musashi, Miyamoto (1982). *The Book of the Five Rings*. New York, NY: Bantam Books, Inc.

Nichols, Annie (2000). "Blockbuster Inc. Adopts Franklin Covey Solutions to Increase Pro- ductivity Amid Explosive Growth." Success Stories. http://franklincovey.com/stories/blockbuster_cs.html [2000].

Noel, Melvina (1997). "Morality in Education." Historical Material; Informational analyses; Position paper.

Reynolds, J.C. (1998). "Do Rural Schools Need Character Education?" Rural Educator, 20, n2, 33-35.

Schaeffer, E. (1999, Oct. 13). "National Character Education Advocate Encourages Increased Federal Support for

Character Education in Public Schools." The Character Education Partner- ship. Http//www.character.org/pr/index.cgi?main [2000, April 25]

Selye, H. (1976). *The Stress of Life*. Revised Edition. New York, NY: McGraw-Hill Book Co.

Shechtman, Morrie & Arleah (2004). *Love in the Present Tense: How to Have A Low-Maintenance High-Intimacy Marriage*. Berkeley, CA: Bull Publishing Company.

Stephens, J. (1984). *The Sword of No Sword: Life of the Master Warrior Tesshu*. Boston, MA: Shambhala Publications, Inc.

Talbot, M. (1991). *The Holographic Universe* (pp. 1-81). New York, NY: HarperCollins Publishers.

Ueshiba, Morihei (Trans. Stevens, John) (1992). *The Art of Peace*. Boston, MA: Shambala Publications Inc.

For coaching, consulting and workshops, please contact us at:

www.victoriousmcg.com
victoriousmcg@gmail.com
(919) 297- 8394

CPSIA information can be obtained
at www.ICGtesting.com
Printed in the USA
BVHW040823150620
581303BV00009B/147